Contents

GW00569970

Introduction

Imagine, if you can, Swansea in the latter half of the nineteenth century, a town very different to the city we live in today. The copper-smelting industry had developed rapidly from small beginnings in the 1790s. Other metallurgical industries had become established – lead, zinc, tinplate, iron and steel, as well as sulphur and arsenic – mostly concentrated on the Lower Swansea Valley. The whole area was a forest of chimneys, belching acrid smoke into the atmosphere. At night the furnaces, many of which were kept alight twenty-four hours a day, glowed red and reminded a number of contemporary commentators of the fiery pits of Hell.

Copper, however, was king, giving the town the nickname 'Copperopolis'. The majestic sailing barques that brought the copper ore from South America became symbols of, and synonymous with, Swansea. New docks had been built to accommodate these ships, a canal linked Swansea with the communities and works at the top of the Swansea Valley, while the Tennant Canal linked Swansea with Neath. The North Dock was created by the simple expedient of straightening the River Tawe by digging the New Cut, and then isolating the bend in the river that this left behind to become the dock. At the southern end of this was the North Dock Basin, alongside which was built another Swansea landmark, Weaver's Flour Mill, the first reinforced concrete structure in Europe. There followed the excavating of the South Dock, which became the home of Swansea's trawler fleet and the home of the Fish Market. As the industrialisation of Swansea continued, and the ships that came to the port grew in size, bigger and better facilities were needed. This led to the creation of the Prince of Wales Dock at Fabian Bay on the east side of the river, followed by the King's Dock and the Queen's Dock.

Then from the 1840s, Swansea joined the national railway network, with the South Wales Railway connecting the town with Neath and Cardiff, and, ultimately, London. The town's pre-eminent position as the world's leading metallurgical centre meant that railway communication was vital to foster economic success. This meant that the town came to enjoy a plethora of railway lines, with seven terminus stations – more than any other town or city outside London. The Great Western Railway, as successor to the South Wales Railway, had its terminus at High Street station. The London & North Western Railway, as successor to the Llanelly Railway, had its terminus at Victoria station. The Vale of Neath Railway terminated its line into Swansea at Wind Street. The Midland Railway came into a terminus at St Thomas and the Rhondda & Swansea Bay Railway terminated at Riverside. The Swansea Harbour Trust had extensive lines around Swansea Docks, with a station at East Dock. Perhaps, however, the best known of Swansea's railways was the Mumbles Railway with its terminus at Rutland Street – technically, of course, the Mumbles Railway had another terminus at Mumbles Pier. The Rutland Street terminus was next to the LNWR's Victoria station, and the two lines ran parallel along the seaward side of Oystermouth Road until they reached Blackpill. Here,

4

Cockle women at Sketty, 1861. Traditionally Gower cockle women took their wares to Swansea along Gower Road. At Olchfa Bridge, they would wash their feet in the stream and put their clogs on for the last part of the journey.

the LNWR line turned inland and up the Clyne Valley to Killay, Dunvant, Gowerton, Gorseinon, Grovesend and Pontarddulais. The Mumbles Railway carried on from Blackpill to West Cross, Oystermouth and to the end of the line at Mumbles Pier.

With rapidly growing industry came a rapidly growing population, as workers and their families arrived in Swansea seeking work. Accommodation for these thousands of people was to be a priority, and consequently areas such as St Thomas, Port Tennant, Sandfields, Mount Pleasant, Greenhill and the area around Paxton Street saw new streets of terraced housing. The more affluent moved to Walter's Road and the Uplands, Northampton Place and St Helen's. The wealth that industry brought enabled factory owners to build grand houses to the west of Swansea, such as Sketty Hall, Clyne Castle and Penllergare House. Swansea was a pioneer of slum clearance and municipal housing. Slums around Dyfatty were cleared and new housing at Greenhill replaced them. To the north and east of the town communities were also growing at Landore, Plasmarl, Morriston, Llansamlet and Clydach.

The town centre was also changing, with the streets crammed with shops, all vying for the hard-earned coin in the workers' pockets. Right outside the castle, Castle Street and Castle Bailey Street had always been an area where tradesmen congregated. Wind

Temporary market viewed from St Mary's Church. Some of the walls of the old market survived the Blitz and temporary stalls were erected within those walls. In the background of this photograph is the Plaza Cinema with its five distinctive air vents on the roof. The Tudoresque building near the centre of the picture is the No. 10 Ye Olde Wine Shoppe.

Street had developed from medieval times as a major thoroughfare, full of shops and bustle. The arrival of the first station meant that High Street now came to the fore as a shopping street, developing as a busy street with pubs and hotels as well as a wide range of shops. The building of the market on Oxford Street gave that area a focal point, and it was not long before shops thronged the street, with hotels and a theatre. The centre of the town was a hive of activity, and when, in the 1840s, Plas House on Castle Bailey Street was pulled down and the site redeveloped as Ben Evans department store in 1898, high-class shopping had come to Swansea. In the years leading up to the Second World War, shops in the town generally stayed open until 10 p.m. Some staff, especially the newly recruited, those of lowly status or the unmarried, lived on the top floors above the shops. They could be called on to open up in the mornings and close up at night. A network of trams linked these streets with each other and with the suburbs and some outlying areas.

Two events brought about dramatic change to the townscape of Swansea. In February 1941 the centre of the town was flattened in the Three-night Blitz. Pounded by German bombs, the result was a lunar landscape of bomb craters, rubble and ruins.

Market women, *c.* 1905. This postcard, one of a number of similar ones produced during the early years of the twentieth century, shows a group of women with their produce on display. They were posed inside the market, giving us a good idea what the inside of the market looked like.

The second was simply economic change. The industries that Swansea had relied upon for its prosperity were in decline. Countries elsewhere in the world were able to compete very effectively and slowly the industries went to those countries – Germany, Japan, the USA and latterly China.

After the war, a new town centre arose, clean modern lines replacing the destroyed buildings. Much of that new development remains, although already some has been lost, as the city centre struggles to compete with out-of-town shopping and online retailers. Retail parks at Llansamlet, Morfa and Fforestfach draw people away from the centre, making it harder for the city to entice quality shops into the centre. Progress, it seems, can be an unsympathetic partner. Once a building has outstayed its usefulness, then only demolition and redevelopment await.

I hope this overview has given you a feeling for what the city used to be like. Like all cities, Swansea has changed over the years, sometimes slowly and sometimes forced by events. Some changes are major and traumatic, others small and easily forgotten. I am now going to examine many of the changes that Swansea has seen over the years, and I hope to bring back memories as well as explain, where possible, the reasons for those changes.

I

Industrial Decline

Swansea's very existence depended on its core of traditional industries. Of these, the metallurgical sector dominated, and as a result there was a large coal-mining sector, a thriving port, and an extensive railway system. Supporting these was a busy commercial sector, with banks, shipping agents, law firms, accountants and a host of others. Perhaps the decline and gradual disappearance of this industrial base was the greatest loss Swansea has suffered. Where the chimneys of dozens of works dominated the skyline, now there are trees, shops, car parks, a few light industrial units, a major stadium and a lake. Very little remains of the industries that made Swansea wealthy, although the communities are still there – Morriston, Llansamlet, Landore, Plasmarl etc. still clinging to the valley sides as they have done for more than 200 years.

Why these dramatic changes? If you are the first to develop a manufacturing process, you will enjoy dominance for some years, until someone else invents a better process, or a cheaper method, and so the advantage will shift to them.

Let me, firstly, however, trace a little of the rise and decline of the copper industry in Swansea. Swansea had proved to be an ideal location for the smelting of copper. Although the copper ore came from Cornwall, the need for easily accessible coal gave Swansea the edge over other locations. Here, at the western end of the South Wales coalfield the coal measures came down to the sea. This meant that there was no need to bring coal, at considerable expense, from inland collieries. Swansea's harbour is sheltered, and the river is navigable for several miles upstream. Here, there is a choice of level sites to erect the necessary furnaces and other buildings. The first copper works was opened in 1717, being the Llangyfelach works. These came into the possession of Robert Morris in 1726, and so began a link between Swansea and the Morris family that endured for more than a century. The Vivian family entered the copper industry in 1800 with a copper works at Penclawdd. The large Hafod Copper Works were built by them in 1809, with the family retaining control of it until 1924. Under them, it became the largest copper works in the world, employing over 1,000 people. The Morfa Copper Works was the last to be built in Swansea, in 1835. The sites were adjacent, so it was possible for them to be combined in 1924 under Yorkshire Imperial Metals.

From 1768 copper ore from Anglesey augmented the Cornish copper ore, but in the nineteenth century the output from Anglesey declined. Demand for copper was on the rise worldwide, and new sources of ore were needed. This was found in Chile, Cuba, and, to a lesser extent, Australia, Canada, South Africa and Spain. To reduce transport costs, these countries began supplying partly smelted ore called regulus. As this was the first step in the smelting process, it was natural that these countries would develop their own smelting works. The result was that Swansea's dominance of the copper industry began to wane. After the 1870s when Cornish ore supplies began to decline, and the

Hafod Copper Works, 1810. The development of Swansea as an industrial centre began in earnest in the eighteenth century. The smelting and finishing of metal was possibly the most important activity. This view of the Hafod Copper Works shows the chimneys that were to become commonplace in the Lower Swansea Valley. Notice the Swansea Canal in the foreground.

Hafod Copper Works, c. 1830. This view is similar to the last, with the canal in the foreground. There are many more chimneys now, all belching their fumes into the atmosphere. A wide range of metals were worked here – iron, steel, copper, lead, zinc and tinplate – along with arsenic and sulphur.

Hafod Copper Works, 1900. Another view of this major works. The Lower Swansea Valley was a concentrated industrial area and the land became poisoned as a result of all the different metals and chemicals that were processed there.

countries further afield began developing their own industries, the copper works began to close, the last one being the Hafod-Morfa Copper Works in 1980. The regeneration of the Lower Swansea Valley – which at its height in 1883 was home to 124 works of various types, including twelve copper works – had begun in 1971. Parts of the works still survive and can be seen adjacent to the Landore Park & Ride car park. Work is going on as I write to reclaim and restore as much of the site as possible.

Other metals that were smelted in Swansea included, roughly in order of importance, zinc, lead, arsenic, nickel, silver and gold. Zinc was smelted at Upper Bank from 1838 and at least half a dozen other works opened over the next fifty years. Rail connections were important to these works, so they were concentrated on the eastern side of the valley, close to the Swansea Vale Railway and the South Wales Railway (later GWR). By 1930 they had all closed, bar one, the Swansea Vale Works, which had opened in 1876 and finally closed in 1971. Lead was smelted at the White Rock works from 1870, ending in 1923. Silver was extracted from the lead ore at these works, and also from copper ore at the Hafod works and at Landore. Arsenic was also extracted from copper ore, mainly at works in the Clyne Valley, but also elsewhere. Both cobalt and nickel were produced at the Hafod Isha works, albeit as a separate enterprise from the copper smelting. This had all largely finished by the early twentieth century.

This expertise in the metallurgical industries was to be a major contributory factor in the concentration of the tinplate industry in Swansea and its surrounding area. The first tinplate works in the area, at Upper Forest, opencd in 1845, followed by another eleven. The last to be built in the Lower Swansea Valley were the Aber and the Birchgrove works in 1880. Outside the valley, at the King's Dock, the Baldwins company built the

White Rock, early 1800s. The works at White Rock developed quite early in the nineteenth century. A ferry across the Tawe operated here for many years.

King's Dock works in 1909 and next door the New Elba works in 1925. The bulk of the production from these works was exported to the United States of America, and it was Welsh tinplate that made much of the homestead expansion across the mid-west possible. Kitchen equipment such as plates, cutlery, pots and pans was made from Welsh tinplate, as was the cans for long-tern preservation of food. The growth of the Texas oil industry relied on oil drums made from Welsh tinplate. The Americans themselves were trying to develop their own tinplate industry and in 1891 a tariff – called the McKinley Tariff – was placed on imported tinplate. The result was a dramatic decline in production of tinplate and a depression in the industry, which lasted almost ten years. By the Second World War, it had become clear that the tinplate industry had to be modernised, with the result that many small works closed. Technological changes saw the opening of two new modern strip mills in the area – at Trostre near Llanelli and at Felindre just north of Swansea. The Trostre works are still in existence but the Felindre works have been closed and the site cleared. In the Lower Swansea Valley, the Upper Forest and Worcester works both closed in 1958 and the Duffryn works in 1961. The two works on the King's Dock closed in the early 1970s.

   Coal mining had been long established in the Swansea area, being situated as it was on the western edge of the South Wales coalfield. By the sixteenth century Swansea was the third most successful coal port in the British Isles, exporting coal for use as domestic fuel to the Channel Islands, France and the western counties of England. The ease with which coal could be obtained in the Lower Swansea Valley was a key factor in the growth of the copper-smelting industry there, not to say all the other metallurgical industries too. There were collieries on both the western and the eastern sides of the valley, but as the nineteenth century wore on, so the output from these pits declined. Attention then shifted further west, to collieries around Cockett and Fforestfach, Gorseinon – the most productive part of the district – north Gower, Clyne and Dunvant. At no time did the collieries of the Swansea area challenge those of the Rhondda and Gwent Valleys, where the pits were bigger and generally more productive. The largest of the Swansea collieries – known as Garngoch No. 2 – stood only at 109 in the league table of Glamorganshire collieries! By 1925 the collieries on the western side of the Lower Swansea Valley had closed, mostly due to flooding after the cessation of the

Aeriel view of Hafod, 1960. Here we can see the effects of the industrialisation of more than 150 years on Hafod.

Landore Steelworks site, 1960s. The clearing of the site of the steelworks had begun by the time of this photograph.

Aerial view of Swansea, 1845. From Norman times, the River Tawe had curved at this point, passing close to the castle. The area between the castle and the river was known as the Strand, as indeed it is to this day. In 1845, however, the pressure on the river at this point for the mooring of ships was great, and so the river was straightened by the creation of a cut, and this became the New Cut. The curved section of the river left behind became the North Dock and the North Dock Basin.

Mynydd Newydd Colliery. This colliery opened in Fforestfach in 1843 and closed in 1933. It was unusual, although not unique, in having an underground chapel where regular prayer meetings were held for over eighty years. On Sunday 13 October 1929 the BBC Radio Broadcast Service broadcast a service from the underground chapel. This quite rare real photograph postcard was produced locally and in limited numbers to commemorate the event. (Alan Jones Collection)

pumping of water. On the eastern side of the valley the Llansamlet Collieries closed in 1930 with some of the north Gower pits, such as Berthlwyd and Lynch, carrying on until just before the Second World War. The last pit to be sunk, and also the last to close, in Swansea was Felin Fran, a late comer being opened in 1931 and remaining open until 1965.

Before moving on from discussion of the collieries in Swansea, I want to mention Mynydd Newydd Colliery, which was sited in the Fforestfach area. It was first sunk in 1843, and just missed its century, for it closed in 1933. It was unusual, although not unique I believe, in having an underground chapel where regular prayer meetings were held. On Sunday 13 October 1929 the BBC Radio Broadcast Service broadcast a service from this underground chapel. I am featuring a photograph of the congregation taken from a locally produced postcard. This is a quite rare item and would have been produced in limited numbers by a local photographer.

By the 1970s Swansea had largely lost its traditional industrial base. In 1971 the Lower Swansea Valley Project was launched in an effort to address the industrial dereliction and the enormous environmental damage that had been done to the area. The results can be seen today, with the area now devoted to light industry, warehousing and retail outlets.

Swansea's Docks

Even from medieval times, Swansea was a thriving port, exporting coal and culm and importing a wide variety of foodstuffs, cloth and wine, etc. After 1717, the import of copper ore was added to the list. Bringing the copper ore to the coal made more economic sense than taking the coal to the copper ore. There were quays alongside the river for some 3 miles upriver. There was, however, pressure from shipowners and industrialists for the creation of a float, or wet dock, something that other Bristol Channel ports had invested in early in the nineteenth century. In Swansea, it took time for the discussions surrounding the proposal for a dock alongside the Strand to reach fruition. The River Tawe was straightened with the creation of the New Cut, which opened in 1845, and the bow of the river that was left became the North Dock, which opened in 1852.

While work was progressing on the creation of the North Dock, proposals were being discussed to create another wet dock on the Burrows. Work on this development

North Dock and St Thomas. The North Dock came into operation in 1851, once all the necessary works had been completed to turn it into a functioning dock. In the background of this postcard view of 1905 St Thomas can be seen, probably the most important of Swansea's suburbs at this time.

North Dock lock gates. One of the works carried out was the erection of lock gates, which allowed the efficient transfer of shipping into the dock.

North Dock drawbridge, 1905. This postcard view of the drawbridge has suffered some damp spotting, but nevertheless gives a good idea of the layout of the area around Weaver's. The Weaver's Mill stood on both sides of the road here. At ground level, the road led to a bridge over the Tawe and carried a railway line, tramline, and the road over the river. There was also a high level railway line (seen on the left here) that enabled trains to travel from High Street GWR station to the Paxton Street yard beyond Victoria station.

began in 1852, and despite various problems, including a change of ownership, the new South Dock was opened in 1859. Both of these must count among the lost features of Swansea, as the North Dock closed in 1928, as it became redundant. Only the North Dock Basin was retained for ships mooring at Weaver's Flour Mill. The remainder of the dock became derelict. The South Dock continued in use as it was the base for Swansea's fleet of trawlers, and was the home of the Fish Market. This dock closed in 1969, and was partially filled in. Within around five years, however, its potential was realised when the city council decided that it would be better used as an amenity. The partial infill was removed, and the sea allowed to flow back into the basin and the dock to create a marina for 600 yachts. This was to be the centrepiece of the new Maritime Quarter, with housing, restaurants and other amenities. One of the sheds was left intact to form the heart of the Welsh Maritime Museum.

The North Dock was, however, filled in and became Parc Tawe, a development of retail outlets, a cinema, ten-pin bowling and the showpiece Plantasia attraction, plus ancillary car parking. This has recently undergone a refurbishment to include a drive-through Costa Coffee outlet and new restaurants.

The Prince of Wales Dock opened on the eastern side of the River Tawe in 1882, with the King's Dock and Queen's Dock following in 1909 and 1923. The Prince of Wales Dock has become the heart of the SA1 development of housing, commercial premises and university accommodation. The commercial port of Swansea now comprises of just two docks – the King's Dock and Queen's Dock. While both the South Dock and Prince of Wales Dock still physically exist, their purpose has changed, and so they have to be added to the list of lost features of Swansea. The North Dock, of course, has gone for good, and therefore is most definitely a lost feature of Swansea.

A goods train passing Weaver's. Here a short goods train has left the docks on the east side of the river and is travelling to the goods yard at Victoria station.

This photograph shows the Weaver's Mill building in a dilapidated state, just as demolition is about to begin. The site is now occupied by Sainsbury's supermarket.

Building the South Dock. By the middle of the nineteenth century it became obvious that Swansea needed more dock facilities than the North Dock and the river frontage could provide this. Accordingly, an area just north of the Burrows was chosen as a site for a new dock. The Swansea Dock Company began work in 1852 but ran into financial difficulties.

Accordingly, the Swansea Harbour Trust was formed to take over the work in 1857, and the dock was completed in 1859.

South Dock Fish Market. Shortly after it opened, the Swansea Fish Market moved to the South Dock, and a base was created for the forty or so trawlers that plied their trade from Swansea.

Prince of Wales Dock. As the nineteenth century progressed and the amount of trade being carried out at the Swansea Docks increased, so more dock facilities were needed. Accordingly on the east side of the river, the Prince of Wales Dock was created in 1882. Today it is the heart of the SA1 development with a second marina.

The King's Dock was added in 1909 and is still in use today as the main part of Swansea Docks. This superb photograph shows a chap in a diving suit working on the lock gates. The suit was probably for protection if and when the water came flooding in. The date is not known but I doubt if health and safety considerations would allow this today! (Bob Harris)

3

Railways

As I mentioned earlier, Swansea's dominant position in the metallurgical industries made it a desirable town for railway companies to have a presence. The first to reach the town was the South Wales Railway under its Chief Engineer Isambard Kingdom Brunel. A broad gauge line from London via Cardiff, this line terminated at High Street in Swansea. Although it has undergone a number of changes, it remains the railway station for Swansea.

To the west of Swansea, the Llanelly Railroad & Dock Company had come into existence in 1828, opening as a steam-hauled railway in 1833. The movement of coal in the area proved lucrative for the new railway and it soon prospered. Extensions were added to what was essentially a mineral line, although passenger services were added in the early 1860s. Further expansion brought lines to Carmarthen and into Swansea in 1867, with the line terminating at Victoria station. The Carmarthen and Swansea lines were run as a separate company, although still owned by the Llanelly Railway. This led to problems as the new lines were not profitable, and were later vested in a new company, the Swansea & Carmarthen Railway. This was incorporated in 1871, and the Swansea line was then sold to the LNWR in 1873. Other parts of the network eventually became GWR property.

The line came from Pontarddulais (opened in 1840) with stations at Grovesend, (opened in 1910, closed in 1932), Gorseinon (opened as Loughor Common in 1867, renamed in 1868, and closed in 1964), Gowerton South (opened as Gower Road in 1867, renamed as Gowerton in 1868, as Gowerton South in 1950 and closed in 1964), Dunvant (opened in 1868, closed in 1964), Killay (opened in 1867, closed in 1964), Mumbles Road (opened in 1868, closed in 1964) and Swansea Bay (opened in 1879, closed in 1964). The terminus at Swansea Victoria was opened in 1867 and closed in 1964. The branch line from Gowerton South to Penclawdd was opened in 1867. It is still possible, with a little imagination, to trace the course of this branch out of Gowerton, past the site of the Elba Steelworks and alongside the road to Penclawdd. The station building still survives as a private house, and there are traces of the station platform in situ. The LNWR extended this line to Llanmorlais in 1884, but this, too, closed in 1931. The attraction for having a branch line along this stretch of the north Gower coast was the presence of collieries, a steelworks and the cockle industry.

The closures in 1964 were all as a result of the rationalisation of the railway network by Dr Richard Beeching. Pontarddulais was not closed, and although it has ceased to be a busy junction, as it formerly had been, the station remains in service, albeit in the 'bus stop' style. Today it is still possible to catch a train from Swansea to Llanelli and thence on the Heart of Wales line to Pontarddulais and on to Shrewsbury. The site of Swansea Victoria station is occupied today by the LC2 leisure centre. The trackbed along the seafront has gone, turned into a cycle track, and the bridge at Blackpill, where the line turned inland to go up the Clyne Valley has been demolished. To cycle from the seafront and onto the Clyne Valley cycle path necessitates crossing the Mumbles Road by means

Victoria station. The nationalisation of the railway network under Dr Beeching saw the line between Swansea and Pontarddulais closed in 1964, and with it Victoria station. Once cleared, the site became the home of the Swansea Leisure Centre – now LC2. (Ben Brooksbank)

Interior of Victoria station. No attempt was made to repair the damage to the glass roof following damage during the Blitz, and the skeletal remains were left in place until closure. (Ben Brooksbank)

Exterior of Swansea's Victoria station. This station was the terminus of the Llanelly Railway's line into Swansea. From 1873 it was part of the London & North Western Railway. During the Blitz of the Second World War it suffered the loss of its all-over glass roof, which was never replaced. This photograph dates from the 1950s, around ten years before the line and the station closed.

The high level line between Victoria station and the South Dock. This line came past Weaver's Mill, crossed the bottom of Wind Street, past Victoria station and on to the Paxton Street Depot. (Alan Jones Collection)

Railway bridge at Blackpill. This bridge brought the railway line over the Mumbles Road, and also across the tracks of the Swansea & Mumbles Railway. Something of an iconic structure, it was much photographed. The advertising showed that a number of Midland towns were accessible from this station.

of a pedestrian crossing. In the Clyne Valley it is still possible to see a few remnants of the mining industry that was centred there.

The Swansea Vale Railway began life as a mineral line heading in a north-easterly direction from Swansea, which opened around 1845. Permission to extend to Brynamman was obtained in 1861, with the new line the Swansea Vale Extension Railway opening in 1864. By May of that year a passenger service was established through to Brynamman from the St Thomas terminus station that the company had opened in 1860. Agreement with the Llanelly Railway in late 1864 allowed the through running of trains, and this formed an important route from Swansea to Liverpool. There were stations at Upper Bank, Landore High Level, Morriston East and Glais, all of which closed in 1950 when the line was closed to passengers. The line itself had been purchased by the Midland Railway in 1876, and then became part of the LMS on grouping in 1923.

In 1985 a group of enthusiasts formed the Swansea Vale Railway Society to run 2 miles of track between Upper Bank and Six Pit Junction as a heritage railway. However, by 2007, repeated acts of vandalism and the withdrawal of support by Swansea City Council forced its closure. The site is now being redeveloped with new housing.

There was a high demand for a transport link between Merthyr, Aberdare and the ports of the Swansea Bay area. Coal and the products of the iron industry needed to be taken to Swansea, Neath or Port Talbot for onward shipment. To address this the Vale of Neath Railway built a line linking Aberdare with Neath, which opened in 1851. An extension to Merthyr was opened in 1853. Attention was now centred on reaching the port at Swansea, which was by far the premier port in the region. To enable this to be done, the Vale of Neath Railway sponsored the creation of the Swansea & Neath Railway. The line from Neath to Swansea opened in 1863 with its terminus in Swansea

Railway Station, Killay.

Killay station. Opened in 1867, Killay station served both the village of Killay and the Gower Peninsula. Closed in 1964, some remains, particularly of the platform edge, can still be seen.

Dunvant station. Opened in 1867, Dunvant station served not only the village of Dunvant, but also the collieries in the area.

Dunvant station showing the sidings. Sidings were provided at Dunvant for the colliery wagons that would be loaded and marshalled here. The station closed in 1964. The site is now partly a car parking area, for those who wish to walk down the old trackbed through the Clyne Valley. There are still remnants of the industrial activity in the valley that made the provision of railway services so essential.

Llanmorlais station. The tiny station building can still be seen in this view taken much later. Like Penclawdd, this was closed to passengers in 1931 and to goods in 1957. The track from Gowerton South has largely vanished under farmland, housing and other developments. (Alan Jones Collection)

Gorseinon station. Gorseinon was an important station on the route to the Midlands. Opened in 1867, it was closed in 1964 along with the others on this line.

being a platform on a viaduct at the bottom of Wind Street. Swansea Wind Street station had its booking office and waiting rooms located in the arches of the viaduct beneath the platform. Trains had to reach the station by crossing a drawbridge that carried the line over the locks at the entrance to the North Dock. In 1873 passenger trains on the Vale of Neath Railway stopped using the Wind Street station, and instead ran over GWR metals into High Street station. From 1881, when local services recommenced, the passenger trains terminated at East Dock station, by agreement with the Swansea Harbour Trust.

The most recent railway undertaking to reach Swansea with its lines was the Rhondda & Swansea Bay Railway. Again, the main aim was to bring coal down to the ports of the Swansea Bay area for export or onward transmission around the British coast. The line opened between Treherbert and Port Talbot in 1890. Extending the line to Swansea and Neath took place in 1894 for goods traffic, and in 1895 for passenger traffic. The last part of the journey to Swansea was over the lines of the Swansea Harbour Trust, but in 1899 the R&SBR built a short mile-long track to its own terminus station at Swansea Riverside station. This station closed in 1933, and the whole area around both the East Dock station and Swansea Riverside station became covered in marshalling sidings. These have now largely been abandoned, and the Dan y Graig locomotive shed has been a storage site for Gower Chemicals.

St Thomas station after closure. The SVR was originally created by Act of Parliament in 1845, but was purchased by the Midland Railway in 1876. The line was closed to passengers in 1950, and each of its stations closed that same year. In 1985 a group of enthusiasts formed the Swansea Vale Railway Society, running 2 miles of track between Upper Bank and Six Pit Junction as a heritage railway. However, by 2007, repeated acts of vandalism and the withdrawal of support by Swansea City Council forced its closure. The site is now being redeveloped with new housing.

Much of the evidence for all this railway activity has gone. I have tried to mention as many closed stations as possible, but still have to add Llangyfelach station, which closed in 1924 and Loughor station, which was situated on the GWR main line to Llanelli. The station was closed in 1960 and today there is almost no trace of it having existed at all. From here the main line passed over Loughor Bridge, which was a wooden bridge designed by Brunel. It enabled the line to cross the mouth of the Loughor Estuary, and has recently been replaced as part of the doubling of this section of the line to Llanelli. A section of the original bridge has been preserved on the Carmarthenshire bank of the river. The doubling exercise also affected Gowerton station (formerly Gowerton North), where both platforms are now in use again. Clydach-on-Tawe station opened in 1875 as Cwm Clydach, was renamed in 1901 and closed in 1950.

I must now turn to Swansea's oldest railway – indeed the oldest passenger-carrying railway in the world – the Swansea & Mumbles Railway. Opened in 1804 as the Oystermouth Railway, its main purpose was to carry coal and other minerals from Clyne Valley to the docks at Swansea. In 1807 an innovator named Benjamin French became the first person in the world to promote the carrying of passengers on a railway, and for this his name should be much better known! Between 1827 and 1860 the passenger service was suspended and only occasional shipments of minerals or coal were carried on the railway. The resumed passenger services continued to use horse-drawn carriages, as they had done before 1827, but the pressure was mounting for the adoption of steam traction. After much deliberation, obstruction and objection, a demonstration of the safety of steam power on a railway like the Oystermouth Railway meant that in 1877 steam traction was introduced on the line. Legal niceties and rivalries between two companies led to the bizarre situation when the steam trains of one operator were followed by the horse-drawn carriages of a rival operator. This tangle took years to resolve, with horse-drawn carriages finally disappearing from the line in 1896.

Demolition of the Paxton Street bridge. When the depot at Paxton Street was closed, the bridge that had carried the line over the road was demolished. The area is now the site of the Civic Centre – formerly West Glamorgan County Hall.

Dan y Graig Locomotive Depot. The distinctive building seen in this photograph is still standing and after closure was bought by Gower Chemicals.

Landore High Level station, another SVR station that was opened in 1850 and closed in 1964. The corresponding GWR station, referred to as Landore Low Level, closed in 1954.

Steam locomotives, however, were only in charge of the trains for a relatively few years. The owners of the railway wanted to introduce electric traction, and in 1902 experimented with electric accumulator cars. These were not a success, and it was not until 1924 that moves were again made to electrify the line. After obtaining Parliamentary permission to go ahead, the rival Mumbles Railway and the bus company were combined under one name: the South Wales Transport Company. An electricity substation was built at Blackpill, new electric cars were ordered, and on 1 March 1929 the last steam train made its final run. The following day, the first of the new electric cars emerged from the Rutland Street shed to begin the new era. The new cars were the largest of their type to run on railway lines in the United Kingdom, and were an immediate success. The clean new electric cars helped to make Mumbles a popular residential area, as well as a well-frequented tourist resort.

Local people soon developed a fondness for the distinctive red cars of the Mumbles Railway, and images of them appeared on postcards, calendars, souvenirs and paintings. The railway was to endear itself even more to the local population, as it did not close at all during the Second World War, despite everything that Swansea and the nation suffered. In this it became a symbol of the resilience of the town and its people. It meant that the townsfolk could escape on the train to Mumbles and there enjoy some relief from the threat of bombing.

In 1954 the Mumbles Railway celebrated its 150th anniversary with a parade, programme of events and a luncheon at the Guildhall. Just four years later the

Pontarddulais station is still open, but it is a shadow of its former self, being a simple 'bus stop'-style station. Formerly a busy junction, where the line from Swansea Victoria met the line from Llanelli and West Wales, Pontarddulais was to see a contraction in services with the closure of the former line in 1964. This photograph shows the Llanelli-bound train leaving the station one damp afternoon in 1965.

Llangyfelach station. This GWR station was closed in 1924. (Alan Jones Collection)

Clydach-on-Tawe station. Opened on 1 March 1875 as Cwm Clydach, this station was renamed Clydach-on-Tawe on 1 November 1901. It closed in 1950. (Brian Prouton)

South Wales Transport Company, who were only leasing the line, arranged to buy out the two companies that actually owned it. In October 1958, they became the owners of the line. Some would say that they used dirty tricks and underhand tactics to gain Parliamentary permission to close the line, which they did on 5 January 1960, with the last service train returning to the Rutland Street depot at 12.20 a.m.

The closure was greeted with anger and dismay in Swansea, and despite occasional plans to revive a railway service along the route of the old railway, the Mumbles Railway was lost to Swansea forever.

Steam train on the Mumbles Railway. Horse power gave way to steam at the end of the nineteenth century, and this picture shows the steam train travelling along the Mumbles Road. For a time it had to share the road with motor vehicles, but was moved to a route nearer the sea.

The slip bridge abutments. At the Slip, where it was possible to gain access to the beach, a bridge was provided that crossed the road, the Mumbles Railway track and the tracks of the LNWR line from Victoria to Pontarddulais. Crossing from the beach, the steps brought you to the Bay View public house, public toilets and the entrance to Victoria Park. There are, as I write, rumours that there will be restoration work carried out on the abutments and a new bridge installed.

4

Swansea Constitution Hill
Incline Tramway

Constitution Hill is a steep hill that runs from Hanover Street to Terrace Road. An enterprising company saw opportunity to build a tramway to enable passengers to ride up or down without the exertion of climbing or descending the hill on foot. The Swansea Constitution Hill Incline Tramway Company developed the little line in 1897 with a winding house at the top, which contained two gas engines that operated pulleys to bring the counterbalanced cars either up or down. A loop was provided half way up the hill so that the two cars could pass each other.

The launch proper was on 1 September 1898 – it had opened initially on 27 August but a technical problem closed it on the same day. The line was never profitable, but as the company that owned the line was linked with a housing development taking place at the top of the hill in Mount Pleasant, it remained open until all the houses were sold. It then closed on 3 October 1901, and was sold for scrap. Another Swansea idiosyncracy lost forever.

A tram going to Brynmill. Trams were provided in Swansea by the Swansea Improvements and Tramway Company from 1878 to 1937. Initially horse-drawn trams were used, but from 1900 electric trams came into service, making Swansea the first town in Wales to use electric traction. This photograph shows a double-deck tram on the Brynmill route.

THE UPLANDS, SWANSEA.

3880   ERNEST T. BUSH

A tram in the Uplands. The service began with four routes, which grew to ten by 1913. There were a variety of tramcars in use: double-deck versions for routes with no low bridges, single-deck trams for those with low bridges. Four open-top cars were introduced in 1904, while special low bridge double-deckers were introduced on the Morriston route. Here a double-deck tram heads for the town centre along Gwydr Crescent, Uplands.

Constitution Hill in Swansea is a steep cobbled street off Walter's Road, and leads up to Terrace Road and Mount Pleasant. For a few years either side of the turn of the twentieth century, a bespoke tramway ran up the hill. The cost of running it, however, outweighed the income it generated, and it was closed and sold for scrap.

5

Swansea's Street Tramways

Street Tramways did not come to Swansea until 1870 when a group of businessmen formed the Swansea Tramways Company to promote tramways in the town. This first company failed due to problems with finance, and the fact that many streets would need to be widened to accommodate tramlines. Therefore, in 1873, a new company, called the Swansea Improvements and Tramways Company (SITC), was created to widen the streets, lay out a tramway network, and also establish a music hall and build the pier at Mumbles.

By 1878, they were ready to open their first routes between the centre of town and St Helens and also to Morriston, with a third route to Cwmbwrla being added in 1882. These were served by horse-drawn trams, although three steam-driven trams were used briefly on the Cwmbwrla route, but were unreliable. Once the SITC was taken over by the British Electric Traction Company, the way was clear for the introduction of electric trams. Swansea, therefore, in 1900, became the first town in Wales to adopt electric

This open-top tram is heading for High Street.

trams. The system used mostly single-deck cars as three of the four routes in operation at this time had low bridges.

More routes were added so that by 1913 there were eight regular routes and two occasional routes. Special low-height double-deck cars were introduced to overcome the problem of low bridges. The large number of railway lines in and around the town meant there were a large number of low bridges to contend with. Single deck cars continued on the Port Tennant route as that had the greatest height restrictions.

As the SITC was quite an innovative company, they were frequently upgrading their tramcar stock, which meant that over the years quite a variety of different designs were to be found on the Swansea system. However, in common with many other cities, the general mood was turning against trams as being inflexible and less comfortable than buses, which were enjoying favour as a preferred transport system. Swansea's street tramway system closed on 29 June 1937 and so ranks among the amenities lost to Swansea.

This single-deck tram is passing Weaver's Mill on the route from St Thomas into the town centre. Closure of the tramway system came in 1937. This was part of a UK-wide wave of tramway closures in favour of buses (or trolleybuses in some cities).

6

Swansea Bus Station

The bus station in Singleton Street was a dark and cavernous place that smelt of oil and exhaust fumes. It had large folding doors at either end, and the buses followed a one-way system, going in one end and leaving the other end. Inside there were stands and even a waiting room. United Welsh buses used this bus station as they could not pick up passengers elsewhere in the centre of town. They served the area beyond the town boundaries, such as Gower, the Swansea Valley and Gorseinon. The town itself was the preserve of South Wales Transport.

Swansea bus station. The bus station in Singleton Street was a dark and cavernous place that smelt of oil. It had large folding doors at either end, and the buses followed a one-way system, going in one end and leaving from the other. Inside there were stands, and even a waiting room. United Welsh buses used this bus station, as they could not pick up passengers elsewhere in the centre of town. They served the area beyond the town boundaries such as Gower, the Swansea Valley and Gorseinon. The town was the preserve of the South Wales Transport Company. Once the Quadrant was built, with a new bus station, the old bus station was converted into a Wilkinson's store.

United Welsh Services Ltd was a separate company within the Red and White group. This group owned bus companies across England and Wales, having begun in Monmouthshire in the 1920s. In 1939 eleven companies owned by Red and White in the Swansea area were amalgamated into a single company, which was named United Welsh Services Ltd. With nationalisation becoming a likelihood in the post-war years, Red and White sold their bus operations to the state in 1950. United Welsh continued to operate under its own name until 1971 when it was absorbed into South Wales Transport.

As a boy growing up in Gower in the 1950s and 1960s, travelling into Swansea by bus meant a trip on the United Welsh bus. I believe our route was No. 13. We always considered the United Welsh buses to be more modern and comfortable than the South Wales Transport buses, which had a darker red livery on a fleet of older vehicles – or so it seemed to us!

Before moving on from buses, I am going to draw your attention to the photograph here of a bus stuck under the railway bridge outside the Cuba Hotel on the Strand. It is an interesting image as it shows the Cuba Hotel, which, like several others in Swansea, had a bit of a reputation for rowdiness. It had closed by 1960 and been demolished. Also the photograph shows the railway bridge that crossed the Strand here, and went on to the high level line that eventually ended at Paxton Street depot. The partner photograph shows the relief bus arriving to enable the passengers to continue their journey.

This lovely photograph shows a bus that had managed to get itself stuck under the railway bridge outside the Cuba Hotel on the Strand. The Cuba Hotel, like several others in Swansea, had a bit of a reputation for rowdiness. It had closed by 1960 and has been demolished. (Bob Harris)

Relief bus to the rescue. Help, however, was not long in arriving, and the passengers could now continue their journeys using the relief bus. (Bob Harris)

7

Theatres and Cinemas

The earliest known theatrical performances in Swansea date from 1617, when the town's accounts list hire charges for the Town Hall for use by travelling theatre companies. The Town Hall continued to be the venue for visiting theatrical events right up to the 1770s. It has to be remembered that Swansea at this time was a genteel spa town where well-to-do visitors came to take the waters, including sea bathing. They would ride in their carriages across the sands of Swansea Bay and visit Oystermouth, and maybe visit the ruins of the Norman castle there. These visitors would have expected entertainments and doubtless there were dances, soirees, lectures etc. provided for them. Also, theatrical events would have figured prominently among the attractions.

To continue producing these in the Old Town Hall was quite unsuitable, so, in 1780, the Swansea Theatre was opened in Anchor Court off Wind Street. This was a bold step that was not without its opponents, but the popularity of the theatre won through, and a series of successful seasons followed. There were some hiccups, but the theatre was thriving on the whole, and the decision was made to open bigger and more up-to-date premises. Opened in 1807 the Theatre Royal was situated on the corner of Bank Street (which later became Temple Street) and Goat Street, which today is Castle Gardens and Princess Way. The site is currently the home of Zara, the clothing chain.

Just two years after opening, the manager successfully persuaded Edmund Kean to perform for two seasons before he went away and became a renowned star of the theatre in both Britain and America. The Theatre Royal had a chequered history, veering from successful times to periods of dire financial difficulty. The opening of the Music Hall in Craddock Street in 1864 brought increased competition for the Theatre Royal, and the second half of the nineteenth century saw its fortunes in decline. In 1898 it was closed and demolished and became the site of the David Evans department store.

The Music Hall was renamed in 1881 as the Albert Hall and for a number of years functioned as a concert hall, hosting celebrities such Dame Adelina Patti and Oscar Wilde. It also held the Swansea's memorial concert for Queen Victoria, who had died in 1901. The year 1912 saw another memorial concert, this time for the victims of the sinking of the *Titanic*.

The advent of cinema brought a new lease of life to the old building, and in the 1920s new sound equipment was fitted and a new projection box was installed. It was, for the next fifty years, the leading cinema in Swansea, but closed in 1977 and was taken over by the Rank Organisation to reopen the following year as a bingo hall. Mecca subsequently took over, but by 2007 had closed. Another lost amenity, although in this case the building still stands, boarded up and neglected.

Meanwhile, in Wind Street the Star Inn was demolished in the late 1850s and was replaced by a wooden amphitheatre, which was rather grandly called the Prince of Wales Amphitheatre. It did not, it would seem, live up to its august name. It hosted

Palace Theatre. Swansea and its surrounding area was well-supplied with places of entertainment. One that has survived, although as a derelict building, is the Palace Theatre in High Street. Opened in 1888 as the Pavilion Theatre of Varieties, it was renamed the Empire Theatre in 1892, and in 1901 became the Palace Theatre of Varieties. It began screening films as part of its programme in 1908, which led in 1912 to it being called Swansea Popular Picture Hall and People's Palace. The year 1923 saw it returned to live theatre and to being the Palace Theatre of Varieties. Then in 1937 it was a cinema again, being called the New Palace Cinema, then just the Palace Cinema. Returning to live theatre again in 1954, it was in 1960 that Sir Anthony Hopkins first trod the boards as a professional performer. After a few years, it became a bingo hall, then a private club and then a nightclub before finally closing in 2007.

Star Theatre, Wind Street. This theatre, at the lower end of Wind Street, was owned and operated by the impresario Andrew Melville, until his death in 1896. Management of the theatre was then vested in Melville's fifteen-year-old-son, also called Andrew, who continued for a short time before William Coutts took over the day-to-day running of the establishment.

Swansea's Theatre Royal, Bank Street, opened on 6 July 1807. It experienced mixed fortunes, sometimes enjoying great popularity and sometimes lying unused. Some of the great actors of the day performed there, but the competition was fierce, and in 1869 it was taken over by George Melville, father of Andrew Melville of the Star Theatre. The Theatre Royal was wound down and in 1899 it was closed and demolished.

Situated on Oxford Street, the Empire Theatre was built in 1900 by Oswald Stoll. It was closed in 1957 and demolished in 1960. A branch of Poundstretcher occupies the site at the time of writing.

The Albert Hall. Opened in 1864 as the Music Hall, Swansea, in 1882 the name was changed to the Albert Hall. Cinema arrived in 1914, with changes being made from around 1929 to accommodate 'the Talkies'. In 1977 new owners Rank closed the cinema. Renovation and refurbishment work began on the building almost immediately and in 1978 it was opened as a bingo hall. Thus it remained for the next thirty years, changing owners in the 1990s when Mecca took over. In 2007, however, the last calls were made and the bingo hall was closed. The building was boarded and remains abandoned.

all sorts of entertainments, and was, on occasions, even called the Swansea Circus, a named that dogged it even after it had been rebuilt in around 1870. In 1872 the local newspaper the *Cambrian* called for its closure as it had had the temerity to allow a female impersonator by the name of Ernest Boulton to perform there. The newspaper considered this to be offensive to public morals.

Taken over by the Melville family in 1874, it was renamed the Star Theatre in 1875, and became for a time Swansea's most popular theatre, with a range of entertainments including musical acts, comedies, tragedies and melodramas. The deaths of two of the Melville family within a few weeks of each other in 1895 saw the Star change hands, being bought by William Coutts, who already had theatre interests elsewhere in Britain. He carried on the successful mix of entertainment that the Melvilles had provided. So profitable was it that he added the Palace Theatre in High Street to his portfolio. This he turned into a cinema, but the Star continued as a live theatre until 1915 when it briefly closed and then reopened as a cinema and was renamed the Royal Theatre. In the 1920s it was used for live theatre again, but with the advent of talking pictures, it was forced to change with the times and in 1931 was rebuilt and reopened as the Rialto Cinema. That survived into the 1960s when it was closed, demolished in 1968 and the site redeveloped. Another long-standing Swansea landmark was lost.

Swansea had, although not concurrently, two Empire theatres. One had begun life in 1888 as the Pavilion Music Hall & Theatre of Varieties and was situated on a triangular site near High Street station. In 1892 Oswald Stoll took over the Pavilion and renamed it the Empire Palace, which was shortened by everyone to the Empire. The Empire attracted many big names, such as Marie Lloyd, George Robey and Dan Leno. However, in 1900 Oswald Stoll opened a new theatre in Oxford Street, and took the name Empire with him. This new Empire Theatre was bigger, more modern and much more elegant. All the big names coming to Swansea from now on performed at the Oxford Street Empire. The High Street Empire changed owners, and changed its name to the Palace Theatre of Varieties. The competition for these new owners was tough, as the top stars went to the Empire in Oxford Street and the smaller touring companies and the popular melodramas were performing at the Star in Wind Street. Five years of difficult times ensued, but in 1905, the fortunes of the Palace changed. The Star in Wind Street had been taken over by William Coutts and he was able to raise enough funds to buy the Palace as well. With the two theatres now under the same management, it was possible to book attractions that complemented not clashed. In 1912, Coutts bowed to popular demand and began to show films at the Palace, even changing its name to the Palace Bioscope, and, in 1912, the Popular Picture Palace. In the following years, a number of purpose-built cinemas opened in Swansea, drawing the audiences away from the old-fashioned Palace. A period of live theatre followed, which brought popular shows to Swansea. The year 1932, however, saw a return to cinema, working when the place was wired for cinema sound. A fire in 1949 during a film showing caused damage to the backstage area, and although some work was done to make the building safe, it then lay unused for around four years. In 1953 it reopened as a theatre hosting a repertory company, but by 1955 was facing closure again. In this instance it was saved by the Swansea Little Theatre, who made it their home for some six years. It was during this period that Anthony Hopkins made his professional stage debut in a play entitled *Have a Cigarette*.

In 1961 the owners of the theatre decided to close it to make way for office development, but this did not happen. In 1967 the building reopened as a bingo hall, spent a short time as a furniture warehouse, and finally became a nightclub. Closing in 1992, the building now stands abandoned, and although it has not disappeared, its life as a theatre seems to be over and as such has been lost to Swansea.

The Empire Theatre in Oxford Street has already been mentioned, having been opened in 1900 under the ownership of Oswald Stoll. Famous stars came to the Empire to perform in the variety shows that were staged there. Top of the list must be Stan Laurel and Charlie Chaplin, who appeared on the same bill in 1910, although not together. Stan Laurel was part of a Fred Karno touring comedy while Charlie Chaplin was at the top of the bill. Lily Langtry, the 'Jersey Lily' appeared on one occasion in a play called *The Frenchwoman*. Comedians such as Max Miller, Max Wall, Ted Ray and Tommy Trinder all appeared at various times on stage of the Empire.

Early in 1940 a talent show for young performers was held at the Empire. Two young men who took part met at this event, and as a result formed a partnership that endured for many years indeed. Eric Morecambe and Ernie Wise did, indeed, meet at the Swansea Empire. They returned in 1948, still relatively unknown, to take part in the pantomime of that year. By the 1950s television was beginning to take its toll on theatre audiences, and while pantomime still brought in the crowds, the rest of each year saw smaller and smaller audiences. In 1957, the owners of the Empire announced that the theatre would close at the end of the pantomime season, 20 February. So, one of Swansea's best-loved theatres was added to the lost list.

Cinema proved a very popular form of entertainment in Swansea, and as has been seen already, a number of the theatres did also show films. Some became exclusively cinemas for periods in their history. Some did not return to presenting live theatre shows. One such was the Opera House in Morriston. This was opened in 1897 as a theatre and within two years, a new manager had taken over by the name of Alfred Denville. He arranged for some improvements to be made to the facilities, enabling a repertory company, led by himself to take up residence. In 1902 he took the innovative step of producing a pantomime in the Welsh language. As far as is known, this was the first all-Welsh production in a theatre in Swansea. However, there seems to have been other problems besetting the management as Mr Denville and his wife departed quite abruptly in February of that year and the management of the theatre was taken over by a Mr and Mrs Clarke. They operated for just a year, for in 1903 the building and its contents were put up for sale.

At this point in stepped William Coutts, the cinema and theatre impresario. It seems that he bought the building in 1910 and renamed it the Bioscope Hall, which operated as a cine-variety venue. This then became the Picturedrome, and in the 1930s the Regal Cinema, when it was owned by Swansea Cinemas Ltd. This was closed in 1962 and the building was demolished in 1965.

Mumbles, too, had a cinema presence – in fact it was blessed with two cinemas. The first to open was the Kursaal, a tin-roofed building that had been transported in pieces from Ilfracombe, and then constructed like a kit in Oystermouth. From 1913 it was used regularly as a cinema, but had become somewhat dilapidated by the 1930s. The decision had been made to replace it, and in the middle of that decade it was demolished and replaced with a modern cinema building. It functioned as a cinema until the 1960s, when it was closed and converted into an amusement arcade. In 2017 that closed, and the building was demolished with the exception of the façade, which,

Tivoli Cinema, Mumbles. The original Tivoli Cinema was housed in a temporary structure and was open by 1918. Rebuilt in the late 1930s, it finally closed as a cinema in 1964. The building became a bingo hall, and later housed an amusement arcade. Today the much-renovated façade remains as the front of a Co-operative supermarket. The rear of the building was demolished and rebuilt as part of the Oyster Walk development of restaurants. A second cinema – the Regent – was opened in Newton Road in the 1920s, but this closed before the Second World War. It is now a short shopping arcade. (Brian Prouton)

after some remedial work, remained. The remainder of the site became a Co-operative supermarket, transferring from the opposite side of the road.

The second Mumbles cinema opened in Newton Road in 1926 as the New Cinema and then as the Regent Cinema. It closed in 1937, unable to compete with the Tivoli on the seafront. Up until the war the building was a warehouse, and then was used by the Home Guard during hostilities. It became the Casino Ballroom in the 1950s, then in quick succession a nightclub and restaurant, a bingo hall, and once again a nightclub and disco. In the early 1970s it became a short arcade of shops called Castleton Walk.

Tivoli was a popular name locally, as there was a Tivoli Cinema in Gowerton and another in Pontarddulais. These were both run by a Harry Thomas, who owned or ran several Tivolis across South Wales. The Tivoli in Cwmbwrla, however, began life as part of the empire of William Coutt, and was a cinema from 1912 through to the 1960s when it was closed and demolished.

The Tivoli in Gowerton opened in 1911 as a cine-variety theatre, on a site close to the LMS railway station (Gowerton South). Its use as a variety theatre was brief as by the beginning of the First World War, it was being used exclusively for film shows. The building was destroyed by fire in 1941, and remained a burnt-out ruin for some ten years. It was rebuilt in the early 1950s but had closed by the early 1970s.

The Tivoli in Pontarddulais opened in 1920 inside the Memorial & Welfare Hall, offering a fare of film, and live performances, with bingo added later. In 1968 the Committee of the Welfare Hall decided to close and the building, including the cinema, then lay empty until it was taken over by a Mr R. H. Scott-Spencer, who reopened it as a hobby during his retirement. The mix of film, live performance and bingo then continued with occasional lettings. The enterprise closed in 1983.

Another 1911 opening was the Gem Cinema in Morriston. This was destined to struggle for forty years, as its rival the Picturedrome (later the Regal) was considered to be a far superior establishment.

Landore Cinema. Opened in 1913, this cinema was closed by 1945. The building is now being used as the Boss Brewery.

The year 1913 saw the opening of the Landore Cinema, which had been specially built as a cinema. In 1937 it was taken over by Swansea Cinemas Ltd, who also owned the Regal Cinema in Morriston. It was closed during the Second World War, but never reopened. The building, which still exists and is unmistakeably a cinema building, is now occupied by the Boss Brewery.

Also in 1913, the Globe Theatre opened in Clydach-on-Tawe. It was nicknamed 'The Shed' or 'The Shack' by local people, which may well say something about its construction and appearance. It did, however, have a dance hall and a twelve-table snooker hall incorporated. The First World War years saw the Globe flourishing, but then in 1921 the building burnt down. It was rebuilt but was then used virtually exclusively as a cinema until it was closed in 1986 and the building abandoned. The building was damaged by fire in 2002 and again in 2004, and the decision was made to demolition it.

The year 1913 was a good year for cinema openings in Swansea with the Pictorium opening in St Thomas and the Castle Cinema opening in the centre of town. The Pictorium was built where Pentreguinea Road joins Morris Lane and by the 1930s was known as the Scala Cinema, and was owned by Swansea Cinemas Ltd. In 1934 it was closed as a cinema. During the Second World War the building was devoted to community use as a British Restaurant. From 1950, for some twenty years, it was used as a tyre warehouse, and was demolished in 1978 as part of a scheme to improve the road layout in the area.

The Castle Cinema was opened on a site at the end of Worcester Place, next to the then offices of the *South Wales Evening Post*. It had the distinction of being the first purpose-built cinema to open in Swansea. In 1967 a comprehensive renovation and modernisation was undertaken. Over the next fifteen years it, like the Elysium before it, turned to soft-porn films as a way of keeping going, but it nonetheless closed in 1982. Circle Cinemas took it over and reopened it as Swansea Film Centre in 1983 with upgraded facilities. It finally closed in 1991 and was turned into Lazer Zone, in which guise it still functions.

In 1914 an imposing new cinema was built in Oxford Street, next door to the Empire Theatre. Named the Carlton Cinema de Luxe, it also boasted a first-floor café, which was popular during the First World War and throughout the 1920s. The elaborate façade of the cinema was granted Grade II listed building status, which meant that it could not be demolished after its closure in October 1977. The bookshop chain Waterstones acquired the building and preserved the façade and the grand staircase but demolished the remainder of the building and created a bookshop and café.

The year 1914 brought cinema to the Uplands with the opening of the Grove Picture House on the corner of The Grove and Gower Road. It later adopted the name Uplands Cinema, and was the haunt of a young Dylan Thomas. Not surprisingly, he does mention going to the Saturday matinees in his writings. It did not have a very long life, closing in 1939 and subsequently being demolished to make way for a branch of Lloyds Bank. That. too, has now closed, and the premises have become a tanning studio.

Also in 1914, the Elysium Theatre opened on High Street not far from High Street station. The cinema was a two-floor venue with a small stage that allowed some variety or music hall acts to perform there. The cinema shared the accommodation with the Swansea Dock Workers Hall and Workingmen's Club. The cinema had gained a somewhat seedy reputation by the middle of the 1950s, showing films of a rather unsavoury nature. In 1960 the cinema closed and was converted to use as a bingo hall.

Carlton Restaurant, Swansea. R. E. Jones, Ltd.

Carlton Cinema and Restaurant. Opened in 1914, the Carlton Cinema had an impressive façade, with a bay window behind which stairs would take the cinemagoer to the first and second floors, and to the Carlton Restaurant. By the 1970s the interior was looking a bit careworn, and it closed in 1977.

Elysium Cinema, High Street. This cinema opened on 11 April 1914, in a building on High Street that it shared with the Swansea Dock Workers Hall and Institute. This dual use continued throughout the life of the building. It survived the Blitz but the cinema was faced with declining audiences in the post-war years, and closed in 1960. The Labour Hall continued in use, and briefly the Elysium was opened as a bingo hall. However, again, a decline in attendances brought about the closure of the bingo hall in 1994, with the whole building, now in a dilapidated state, closed in 1998. The building still stands, but is boarded up and decaying rapidly. The arcade on the left is actually a mural painted by staff and students of Swansea Art College.

Some parts of the building continued to be used by the Labour Party as offices until 1994, when both parts were closed and boarded up. The building still survives but is in a parlous state of repair.

The 1920s and the new Manor Cinema opened in Bohun Street, Manselton, with its art deco façade. This was a purpose-built cinema that was closed for the duration of the Second World War, reopened in 1947 and then remained in use as a cinema until around 1967 when it made the switch to being a bingo hall. Finally closing in 1997 or thereabouts, it was then demolished and the site used for a housing development.

Next to open, in 1931, was the Plaza Cinema at the eastern end of St Helen's Road (after the war, this became part of the Kingsway). It was the largest cinema in Wales at this time and it boasted a top-quality cinema organ. On the first floor, there was a palm-court restaurant with a pianist playing at lunchtime and in the evenings. In 1953 it was fitted with CinemaScope and stereophonic sound, being the first independent cinema in Britain to be so equipped.

Oceana. The Odeon closed to enable the building to be converted into nightclub called Oceana. That, too, has now closed, and the site is awaiting redevelopment. At one time rumours abounded that it was to become the home of the new Central Library. (*South Wales Evening Post*)

Odeon Cinema, Sketty. Opened in 1938 originally as the Maxime, and later taken over by the Odeon group, the cinema closed in 1962. The façade survives but the rest of the building was demolished and rebuilt as sheltered accommodation for the elderly.

It closed in 1965, and was demolished to make way for a new cinema – the Odeon. The cinema was on the first floor of the new building, with a supermarket and other shops at ground level. In 1982 it was divided into three screens. Despite being refurbished in 1995, the Odeon closed in 1997. The space was divided into bars and a nightclub, and became Oceana nightclub before it final demolition in 2017. At the time of writing the site has not been developed and there is considerable speculation as to what use it will be put.

The year 1938 saw two new cinemas open: the Tower Cinema in Townhill and the Maxime Cinema in Sketty. The Tower survived as a cinema until 1963, when it became a bingo hall and dance club. Having closed in 1986, the building was boarded up and left unused for some six years. Arsonists set fire to it in 1992 and this led to it being demolished in 1994. The Maxime in Sketty enjoyed better luck. In July 1947 it was renamed the Odeon, as it had become part of the Odeon Theatre Group. As with so many cinemas and theatre, however, it became a bingo hall as part of the Top Rank Bingo organisation. It passed to Mecca Bingo before closing in 1995. Much of the building remains intact, as only the cinema element was demolished to enable sheltered accommodation for elderly people to be built. This took the name Maxime Court, so harking back to the original name of the cinema.

To complete the list of cinemas that were open at one time or another in Swansea, I just need to mention two about which very little is known: the Olympic Cinema in Lower Oxford Street, which opened in 1912, and the Electric Cinema in Union Street, which opened in 1913 and occupied No. 13. Closure dates for these two establishments are not known. Another about which only a little is known was the Dolphin Cinema in Clydach-on-Tawe. This opened before 1924 and was still functioning a year or so later, probably as a cine-variety theatre.

Fforestfach had its Welfare Cinema in the Welfare Hall, which had opened in 1928 and was being used regularly for cinema showings in the 1940s. The cinema here closed in April 1976 and was one of the last of the cinemas to close in the suburbs of Swansea. It reopened as a bingo hall, and then became a snooker hall. Subsequently the building was demolished and replaced with a short run of shops.

The year 1977 saw a late arrival to the pantheon of Swansea's cinemas with the opening of the Studio Cinema at the bottom of St Helen's Road near its junction with Brynymor Road, an area that for many years was called Hospital Square. The redundant St Paul's Church was deconsecrated and turned into the Studio Cinema with two screens. A third screen was added later, but the enterprise never really thrived and closed in 1989. The building remained empty through much of the 1990s until it was converted into an Indian restaurant called Miah's at the end of that decade. That has now closed, and the building once again stands empty.

St Paul's Church. This redundant church became the Studio Cinema with eventually three screens. The venture was not especially successful and closed. After a period as an Indian restaurant, the building is now empty and beginning to show signs of vandalism.

8

Hotels and Public Houses

As the nineteenth century drew to a close, and the twentieth century made its first faltering steps on to the stage of world history, Swansea was blessed with 228 public houses. On top of that were a number of hotels – not surprising for a busy, wealthy town. Visitors needed somewhere to rest their heads, and the working folk needed somewhere to slake their thirsts. I will not be able to list them all, but I will begin this section by mentioning three breweries that operated in Swansea. William Hancock had a large brewery on Little Wind Street, and were an established supplier of beer to many of Swansea's public houses. The Swansea Old Brewery was established in 1896 on Singleton Street, was acquired by Hancocks in 1927 and brewing ceased there in 1934. Thomas Jones' High Street brewery was an old established business when it was acquired by Hancocks in 1891 and then closed in 1894. Hancocks were able to add thirteen public houses to the ones they already ran in Swansea as a result of this purchase. However, the brewery on Little Wind Street had become outdated and was closed and the site cleared for a new development, called at the time Salubrious Place. In 2018 this name was changed to City Gates.

So many of Swansea's hotels and public houses have been lost that it would be impossible to include the story of each one. Instead I will list just some of those that have either gone completely, are being used today for a different purpose, or are just sitting closed and boarded up, awaiting their fate. I hope that some of these names will bring nostalgic memories for many readers. Let us begin with a tragedy.

The Mackworth Arms Hotel stood on Wind Street, and was a coaching inn of some renown. Anyone travelling by mail coach or stagecoach to Swansea would end their journey at the Mackworth Arms and many would stay at the hotel. The hotel had a number of famous visitors including Admiral Lord Nelson, who stayed there with Sir William and Lady Hamilton in 1802. The painter J. M. W. Turner also stayed at one time. We, though, are concerned with a twenty-two-year-old woman who came to Swansea in 1816 and took a first floor room. Her name was Fanny Imlay and she was the sister of Mary Shelley, the daughter of Mary Woollstonecraft and sister-in-law of Percy Bysshe Shelley. Her family was, however, quite dysfunctional. Mary Wollstonecraft had had her out of wedlock, and they both had been abandoned by Fanny's natural father, a fellow called Gilbert Imlay. Mary then married a man called William Godwin, who was the father of Mary Shelley. Unfortunately she died giving birth to Mary. Godwin then married a woman called Clairmont, who had two children of her own, both by different fathers. Shelley then left his pregnant wife and fled with Mary, who was sixteen years old at the time. Fanny found the scandalous behaviour and bohemian lifestyle of the family too much to bear. In October 1816 Fanny took the mail coach to Gloucester, stopping briefly to post letters at Bristol, one of which was to her sister in Bath. She then took the Cambrian coach to Swansea. Arriving at the Mackworth Arms, she took a first-floor room and instructed the staff she was not to be disturbed. She then took a fatal dose of laudanum. In this she was, perhaps unconsciously, copying her own mother, who had attempted suicide in 1795 in the same way. Both Mary Shelley and Percy Shelley rushed to Swansea on Mary's receipt of Fanny's letter. They proved to be too late to prevent the tragedy.

Although the Mackworth Arms Hotel was demolished in the 1890s and replaced by the new Head Post Office building, there are still reports of unexplained noises and the ghostly presence of a young woman. Perhaps Fanny Imlay is truly haunting Swansea.

Richard Edwin Jones was an entrepreneur in the hospitality business that he launched in the 1870s in Cardiff and which grew from the one café into a multi-million-pound empire. By 1890, he felt the lure of Swansea and desired to build a grand hotel in the town. He purchased a site in High Street, and then purchased the name, goodwill and equipment of the Mackworth Arms when it was demolished. In 1895 his new Mackworth Hotel opened at Nos 41–44 High Street. It was a grand Victorian edifice with balconies, shops on the ground floor, an in-house bakery and a wine merchants, both of which were open to the public. There was a six-table (which later became twelve) billiard room, a resident orchestra and a novelty for the times – an automatic café. This had been copied from similar establishments in Berlin, and was a forerunner of self-service cafés and fast-food outlets.

During the Second World War the hotel escaped damage during the Blitz and provided accommodation for Vera Lynn when she was performing in the town. In 1952 Laurel and Hardy stayed at the Mackworth while they were appearing at the Empire Theatre.

In 1957 a man by the name of Gerald Lamarque murdered his wife's lover, by the name of Eric Batty, and the manager of the hotel with a sheath knife that he had purchased for the purpose. It transpired that Lamarque had been a spy during the Second World War using the name Allerton as a false identity, and had been something of a hero. While imprisoned he wrote a number of popular wartime adventure stories using the non-de-plume 'Zeno'. The identity of 'Zeno' was to remain a secret for many years until Lamarque's widow (his second wife) began to receive death threats and went to the police. The whole story then came out into the open and the facts that had been kept secret for so long were laid bare. The murder, however, had an adverse affect on the reputation of the Mackworth Hotel, and it closed in 1967. It was demolished in 1971.

Another well-known hotel on High Street was the Bush Hotel, a Georgian building that stood on the site of an earlier hostelry that had hosted Oliver Cromwell. It was demolished in 2013. Also on High Street, the Cameron Hotel, originally the Cameron Arms, was known to be in existence in 1840 when it was used for a Masonic meeting – incidentally they had also used the Mackworth in Wind Street in 1871. It was a well-known landmark on High Street up until 1927 when it was purchased by F. W. Woolworth Ltd and demolished to make way for their first Swansea store. It is worth remembering that Woolworths had two stores in Swansea, the other being on Oxford Street.

High Street had other well-known hostelries including the Shoulder of Mutton, next door to the Elysium Cinema. This still stands but has been empty for several years and is now boarded up and abandoned. Nearby is the Adam & Eve, another well-known establishment that is now closed and locked up (see image on page 50).

The demolition of the Mackworth Arms Hotel in 1898 briefly left Wind Street lacking a top-class hotel. Consequently the George Inn was demolished in the early 1900s, and in its place rose the Metropole Hotel. Sadly this joined the lost list in 1941 when it was destroyed during the Blitz.

Another one-time Wind Street fixture that has now joined the lost list is The Adelphi Hotel. Opened after 1854, The Adelphi was a popular venue for society dinners and celebratory events. It was, at various times, known by other names, but in the year 2000 reverted to its old name. It finally closed in 2016. Throughout the Second World War it was popular with servicemen, especially US soldiers who were based locally in the run up to the D-Day landings. One such was a young Rocco Marciano. One night he had come along to The Adelphi with a group of friends and characteristically ordered a glass of milk. An Australian sergeant noticed this and began taunting Rocky. Shall we just say that the Australian soon regretted his error of judgement.

Back in High Street, another fixture was the Great Western Hotel, which sat at the corner of High Street and Alexandra Road. In the 1890s it was a temperance hotel, forbidding the sale of alcoholic beverages. Despite this, or maybe because of it, it was a busy and popular hotel. It survived the Blitz and continued in existence until 1974, when there were plans to demolish it and replace it with a modern hotel. These came to nothing and while the hotel was demolished, it was replaced with the very large office block we know as Alexandra House. The demolition also encompassed the neighbouring buildings, which included the Alexandra Arcade, where Marks & Spencer had established their first shop in Swansea.

From Masonic records we know that there were two hostelries on the Strand that had been venues for their meetings: The Fountain Inn was used in 1805 and again in 1817, and the Tiger Inn was also used in 1805. The Strand, at this time, was one of the main thoroughfares in Swansea, running as it did alongside the river. How salubrious the area was at this time we cannot say, but both the Fountain and the Tiger must have been of a reasonable standard for the Masons to use them for meetings. The Cardiff Arms was also sited in the Strand, and had opened before 1850. It was rebuilt probably in the middle of the twentieth century, but had closed by 1993. Like a number of empty Swansea public houses, it was destroyed by fire in the early 2000s. Another, probably later, hotel on the Strand was called the Arches Hotel, which was positioned opposite the arches of the high level railway line. These arches were occupied by a variety of businesses.

In 1813, the Masons met in the Cambrian Hotel in the Burrows area, which would have been considered a better class of area by most of Swansea society. Another hotel in this area of town was the Burrows Inn, situated in Adelaide Street. I do not know its fate.

The Old Swan Hotel, an old established hotel, was situated on the corner of Dynevor Place and Gower Street. It suffered severe damage during the Blitz and the site was later cleared. Gower Street became part of the Kingsway, and the site is now occupied by the Dragon Hotel. Another long-established hotel was the Longlands Hotel on St Helen's Road. The site was acquired by the Swansea YMCA and a new building was erected by them in 1911. That building still stands.

Situated in Rutland Street, the London & North Western Hotel was close to Swansea's Victoria station. This was the terminus of the London & North Western Railway until 1922, hence the hotel's name. It was a victim of German bombs during

Arches Hotel, Strand. This is a particularly interesting photograph of the lower end of the Strand. The Arches Hotel is situated in the centre of the buildings facing the high level railway line. In the distance Weaver's Mill can be seen. The arches of the railway viaduct are all occupied by various businesses, and there is a general air of purposeful activity. Note, also, the single-deck tram travelling up the Strand.

JACK EVANS, Proprietor, OLD SWAN HOTEL, Gower Street, SWANSEA. *Jack Lewis, Polytechnic Studio, Swansea.*

Old Swan Hotel, Gower Street. This old established hotel was situated on the corner of Dynevor Place and Gower Street. It suffered severe damage during the Blitz and the site was cleared. Gower Street became part of The Kingsway and the site is now occupied by the Dragon Hotel.

LONGLANDS HOTEL, ST. HELEN'S ROAD, SWANSEA. BURROW, PUBLISHER, CHELTENHAM

Longlands Hotel, St Helen's Road, another long-established hotel that had closed by 1911. The Swansea YMCA acquired the site in that year and built the YMCA building that still stands today.

the Blitz in 1941. After the war, the Terminus was opened in the area, again reflecting its nearness to the station. This survived until 1994 when it was closed, and then became an Indian restaurant.

The centre of Swansea had a number of public houses. The Exeter Hotel in Oxford Street was situated opposite the market. Opened in the 1870s, it features on many postcards from the early years of the twentieth century. Unfortunately it was damaged during the Blitz and was subsequently demolished. The Three Lamps was on Temple Street, and said to have been a favoured haunt of Dylan Thomas. This could easily be true as it was only round the corner from the Kardomah Café in Castle Street. Destroyed in the Blitz, it reappeared in roughly the same spot after the war. Temple Street had gone by this time, and the pedestrianised walk that replaced it was part of Castle Square. The Three Lamps became The Office through the 1990s and 2000s, but, just as I write, it has reverted to its old name.

In Union Street, the No. 10 Ye Old Wine Shoppe, a mock-Tudor building on three floors, was reputed to be another Dylan Thomas haunt, and he does mention the establishment in some of his writings. A feature of the No. 10 was a stuffed, 8-feet-tall Bavarian dancing bear by the name of Boris. It is said that the unfortunate bear died while in Swansea on tour in the 1890s. There are possibly apocryphal stories that Jimi Hendrix visited Swansea in the 1960s and was photographed with Boris. The No. 10 closed in 1988, and is now a health food shop.

Also in Union Street was the Music Hall Hotel, so called for its proximity to the Albert Hall, which had been called the Music Hall when it was originally opened. This establishment is worthy of note because of a tragedy that occurred in 1876. Mr Jenkins,

London & North Western Hotel. This establishment got its name from the fact that it was situated in Rutland Street, almost adjacent to Swansea Victoria station, which of course was operated by the London & North Western Railway until 1922. Evidently it changed its name to The Clyne Valley Hotel in 1941.

Terminus pub. Situated near the Rutland Street terminus of the Mumbles Railway and the Victoria station terminus of the old LNWR line, it could be said to have been named for either. Built after the Second World War, it closed in 1994.

Exeter Hotel, Oxford Street. Situated opposite the market, the Exeter Hotel was opened in the 1870s. It suffered damage during the Blitz and was subsequently demolished.

the landlord of the hotel, was walking in Oxford Street when he slipped on a piece of discarded orange peel. Sustaining severe head injuries, he died a few days later. His was not the only death in Swansea from orange peel. Another happened in 1904 and a third in 1905. Injuries were many as a result of pedestrians slipping on orange peel thrown down quite deliberately.

The New York public house was a feature of the lower southern end of Princess Way for many years and was instantly recognisable in its red and gold livery. Now closed, it has become the No. 6 restaurant.

The Sandfields area of Swansea, which lies roughly between the town centre and the Guildhall, was the proud home of the Vetch Field, where Swansea Town (later Swansea City) played their home games. On match days hundreds of fans would descend on the area and its numerous pubs. The match-day trade kept these places afloat, so when on 30 April 2004 the last football league game was played there, so an era came to an end.

The move from the Vetch Field proved catastrophic for the pubs in the Sandfields. The bulk of their trade had now gone, as they could no longer top up takings on match days. Most closed within a few years. Here I will mention just two: The Garibaldi Inn, which had a fearsome reputation, and The Brooklands Hotel, which was on the edge of the Sandfields near Brynymor Road, and, I believe, latterly served real ale. It closed around 2012.

Down on Oystermouth Road, next to the gasworks site, which is now the Swansea Marina branch of Tesco, was the London Inn. This end of terrace pub would have served the workers from both the gasworks and the railways that passed its door. In the

Brooklands Hotel. I have not been able to find out very much about this particular pub. I have been told that it was a typical example of a town pub of its type. I believe it sold real ale at one time. Closed around 2012, it became an office for a building company, but without any dramatic changes being made.

late 1980s it was being run as a Truman's pub, but closed soon after and reopened as the Swansea Jack, named after a famed, heroic local dog. It is now closed and boarded up.

Before leaving the town centre, I am going to mention just a few more of the pubs that have closed there: The Burrows Inn in Adelaide Street; the Somerset Hotel and the Centre Hotel, both in Somerset Place and both, I believe, demolished in the 1960s; The Colosseum Hotel on the corner of Little Wind Street and Wind Street, roughly where TGI Fridays now trades; and the Belle Vue Hotel in Nelson Street, which became the Quadrant Gate when the new shopping centre was built, and has since closed and been converted in several shop units. Some that I understand were all destroyed in the Blitz include Albion Inn, Nelson Street; Royal Albert Inn, Orange Street; Bridge Inn, St Thomas; Druids Arms, Lower Orchard Street; General Picton, Orchard Street; The Oystermouth, Paxton Street; Mansel Arms, Oxford Street; and the Duke Hotel, Wind Street.

Moving out of the town centre down to Mumbles, we find the Antelope has now gone, as has the Kinsale Irish Pub. The latter's building has only been closed and locked up, which cannot be said of the much older Ship & Castle. This was opened in the nineteenth century and suffered a disastrous fire in 1896 after which it was rebuilt.

Burrows Inn, Adelaide Street, an old establishment that got its name from its location in the Burrows area of Swansea.

London Inn, Oystermouth Road. An end-of-terrace pub, it would have served railway workers and workers from the adjacent gasworks. At the time that this photograph was taken (probably in the late 1980s) it was being run as a Truman's pub. (Alan Jones Collection)

Swansea Jack, Oystermouth Road. The London Inn became the Swansea Jack, taking its name from the famed dog of that name, probably in the early 2000s. It is now closed and boarded up.

It closed permanently in 1927, however, for being a 'disorderly house', which, of course, is a euphemism for being a brothel. It is now the site of the Mumbles Conservative Club.

Also in Mumbles, we had the Mermaid Hotel. This hostelry had a long history, having been in existence during the Napoleonic Wars when it was called the New Mermaid. The landlady at the time was a Mrs Stephens, whose husband had drowned at sea in 1791 and whose son died in France after eight years' incarceration at the hands of the French. Rebuilt in 1898, it was another of the drinking haunts of Dylan Thomas. It was demolished in 1996 after a fire.

Before leaving Mumbles, I must mention the Kinsale Irish Pub on Western Lane, which is a very recent closure. Also the Rock & Fountain at Newton and the Linden Tree in West Cross have been quite recently closed.

Heading from Mumbles out to the Gower bays, a number of hotels have vanished from the landscape. Among them was the Langland Court Hotel, a one-time favourite for wedding receptions. Opened in 1884, it closed in 2002 and was destroyed by fire in 2005. The site has been developed for housing. At Rotherslade, the Osborne Hotel opened at the end of the nineteenth century. One early distinguished guest was the French impressionist painter Alfred Sisley. Another was James Callaghan, although not while he was prime minister. The hotel was closed in 2001 and then demolished between 2003 and 2004. It was redeveloped as a block of flats called Osborne Court.

Before we mention the pubs in Gower that have closed, I must add the Bush in Sketty, a mock-Tudor building that has dominated Sketty Cross for many years. Closed as a pub in 2008, it is now occupied by Viney Hearing Care. Also let us not forget the

Osborne Hotel, Rotherslade. Originally opened towards the end of the nineteenth century, one early distinguished guest was Alfred Sisley, the French impressionist painter. Another distinguished guest was James Callaghan, though not while he was prime minister. It was closed in 2001 and was demolished between 2003 and 2004. The site was redeveloped as a block of flats called Osborne Court.

Langland Bay Hotel. Built in the nineteenth century by the Crawshay family of Merthyr Tydfil, the building became a hotel in the early twentieth century, and then a Convalescent Home for Miners. The building remains and still dominates Langland Bay, but today is home to thirteen luxury apartments.

Mile End Inn on Carmarthen Road. This distinctive building, which is taller than its neighbours, is now three private flats.

In Gower, farewells have been said to the Joiners Arms in Three Crosses, the North Gower Hotel in Llanrhidian and the Greyhound Inn in Old Walls. The Greyhound Inn is boarded up currently, with rumours about housing being built on the site. The Joiners is now closed and locked up, but is advertised as to let, so maybe some enterprising person may feel confident enough to open it up again. The North Gower, however, which was originally a private house built in the 1920s and only became a hotel after the Second World War, closed in 2013 and has been replaced by a small estate of houses.

The Welcome to Gower Inn in Gowerton was a Brains pub that had been struggling for a few years, and despite changes in management, the decision was made to close the doors for the last time. Its site, on a busy crossroads and with only a small car park, may have contributed to its demise. There seems to be no particular plan for its future.

Finally, I want to mention two pubs in Pontarddulais that have closed. The Gwyn Hotel is the last building in Swansea before one crosses the Loughor River into Carmarthenshire. Built in the mid-1880s it was named after the landowner Hywel Gwyn. Its first landlord was Isaac White. Closed at the end of the twentieth century, it became the 'Little India' restaurant. That has also closed, and it now has a hand car wash at the rear in what was the car park. The building itself, I am told, is in a dangerous condition.

The Bush, Sketty Cross. This mock-Tudor building has dominated Sketty Cross for many years. It closed as a pub as recently as 2008 and is now occupied by Viney Hearing Care.

The Greyhound Inn after closure. In 2018 the falling away of trade led to the closure of the pub. This was greeted with considerable sadness as it had been a part of Gower life for so long. It is now empty and boarded up and there is some talk of it being demolished to make way for housing.

Welcome to Gower, Gowerton. This Brain's pub had been struggling for a few years, and despite changes in management, the decision was made to close the doors for the last time. There seems to be no particular plan for its future.

The Gwyn Hotel is the last building in Swansea as one crosses the Loughor River into Carmarthenshire. Built in the mid-1880s, it was named after the landowner Hywel Gwyn. Its first landlord was Isaac White. Closed at the end of the twentieth century, it became the 'Little India' restaurant. That has also closed, and it now has a hand car wash at the rear, in what was the car park. The building itself, I am told, is in a dangerous condition.

The King Hotel is situated on the corner of St Teilo Street and Pentre Road. It closed in 2018, and there are rumours that it will be converted into a Co-operative supermarket.

I am sorry if I have not mentioned your favourite closed Swansea pub. There are very many of them, and each one has stories and memories.

King Hotel, Pontarddulais. Situated on the corner of St Teilo Street and Pentre Road, the King Hotel is a substantial building, yet in 2018 it closed. Rumour has it that it will be converted into a Co-operative supermarket. Pontarddulais did have a Co-operative store further down St Teilo Street, but that closed when Tesco opened up just behind them.

9

The Townscape

Before the Second World War Swansea's town centre was a thriving place with a wide range of shops and, as we have seen, plenty of hotels and public houses. By looking carefully at postcards published around 1905, it is possible to see just how busy High Street, Castle Street, Wind Street and Oxford Street were at that time. All crammed with shops and commercial premises, festooned with advertising boards, bunting and placards, just about every means was used to draw shoppers' attention to products and services.

Ben Evans' department store faced Swansea Castle. Referred to as the 'Harrods of Wales', it was built in 1893 in typically ornate Victorian style. It claimed to have 3 acres of floor space and 600 feet of street frontage. Some members of staff lived in, which was not uncommon for shop staff in the interwar years. Shops tended to stay open until 10 p.m. or later. To have a few staff living in rooms right at the top of the building enabled early openings and late closings that were expected at that time. This practice may not have continued into the war, as shop opening hours were in many cases reduced to free workers up for other duties, like fire-watching or as ARP wardens.

The first major Blitz-type raid on Swansea was on the night of the 1 and 2 September 1940, when thirty-three people were killed as bombs landed all over the town. The second major raid was on 17 January 1941 with serious damage to King's Dock, St Thomas and Hafod. Fifty-Five people died on this occasion. The third of these major raids was the infamous Three-Night Blitz of February 1941, which saw the destruction of Ben Evans' store, Swansea Market and St Mary's Church. Oxford Street shops, Castle Street premises, College Street, Wassail Square and its surrounding streets were comprehensively destroyed, as were premises in Orchard Street, Northampton Place, Goat Street, Gower Street, Park Street, Temple Street, Waterloo Street, Calvert Street, Caer Street and Dynevor Place. The market was gutted by fire and Victoria station was hit, as were properties around South Dock.

Temple Street had gone and with it the David Evans department store, which had been built on the site of the Theatre Royal. Ben Evans department store also had been flattened. Castle Street's western side had been destroyed, although Castle Buildings on the eastern side of the street survived. Among the casualties was the Kardomah Café, which, according to Dylan Thomas, was 'razed to the snow'. 230 people died over these three nights.

Wind Street largely survived, as did the St Helen's Road area, Brynymor Road and most of Sandfields. Mount Pleasant escaped, and Townhill and Mayhill both suffered some damage. The industries of the Lower Swansea Valley were not significantly affected. The brunt of the destruction was in the town centre and it must have gladdened Hitler's heart when he heard that while they could still produce munitions, the people of Swansea could not go shopping!

Castle Lane, 1850. This view of Swansea Castle shows the lane that leads from the Strand, past the side of the castle, to Castle Bailey Street. It is still possible to walk this lane, although the surroundings are completely different today.

Altogether, Swansea suffered forty-four air raids of varying intensity between June 1940 and February 1943. The total death toll was 387, a number that was lower than it might have been had Swansea's air-raid precautions not been particularly effective.

This meant that after the war a huge programme of rebuilding was required to replace the town centre. St Mary's Church was rebuilt using the exact same plans that had been used when it had been restored in the 1890s. The market, which had lost its glass roof, just became a temporary outdoor market until its replacement could be built. Victoria station also lost its glass roof, but the girders holding the roof up had not been destroyed, and so the station remained with no roof until its closure in 1964.

Temple Street, *c.* 1860. This engraving from the middle of the nineteenth century shows the newly built Head Post Office at the top by the castle. On the left-hand side is the Theatre Royal, and on the right is a local bank, although that is not clear to see.

Castle Bailey Street, *c.* 1905. The shops on the right-hand side, in Castle Buildings, which have the rounded windows, survived the Blitz and remain to this day.

Castle Street. This, another postcard view, shows Castle Street curving towards High Street. It is a mass of banners, advertising material and shop awnings. All disappeared as a result of the Blitz.

Buildings in the Strand. These derelict buildings were photographed in the early 2000s. Situated in the Strand, they show how some buildings were extended upwards, incorporating existing brickwork like the chimneys. The recent redevelopment of the Strand saw the demolition of these buildings. (Bob Harris)

Dunvant Place was demolished to make way for the car park of the Civic Centre.

Sloane Street was also demolished to make way for the Civic Centre.

Swansea Gasworks. Situated on Oystermouth Road, these gasworks replaced a smaller one in Dyfatty. Today the site is occupied by the Tesco Marina superstore.

Wassail Square. Frog Street ran along the south side of St Mary's Church, and widened into Wassail Square at its western end. Frog Street was badly damaged in the Blitz, as were a number of buildings in Wassail Square. The development of the Quadrant meant that Wassail Square disappeared.

Worcester Place. This is a narrow street that runs behind Castle Buildings, parallel with Castle Street. In this photograph, it is possible to see the tower of the old Head Post Office on Castle Bailey Street.

Northampton Place. Nothing in this postcard view of Northampton Place survived the Blitz. Today it is the part of The Kingsway that leads into St Helen's Road. The large tree in the centre is masking the YMCA, which was built just before the First World War.

Ben Evans department store, *c.* 1905. This advertising postcard from the beginning of the twentieth century promotes Ben Evans department store, claiming that it has 3 acres of floor space and 600 feet of street frontage. It was situated where Castle Gardens lies today.

Ben Evans department store after the Blitz. The Ben Evans store was completely destroyed as a result of the Blitz in 1941. This meant that one of Swansea's most iconic landmarks had gone.

Shelter in Castle Gardens, 1960s. Once the site previously occupied by Ben Evans department store had been cleared, and as part of the general reconstruction of Swansea, moves were made to create public gardens. Called Castle Gardens, due to their proximity to the castle, the area was laid out with flower beds and footpaths. In the north-west corner a shelter with seats was provided, and it proved very popular with older shoppers. This shelter was removed during a later revamp of the gardens.

Castle Street after post-war remodelling. By the 1960s new shops had been built along the western side of Castle Street. The edge of the new Castle Gardens can just be seen on the left-hand side of the picture.

Before discussing the rebuilding of Swansea town centre after the Blitz, I just want to make mention of RAF Fairwood Common, which was opened on 15 June 1941 as a fighter station in 10 Group of Fighter Command. It had taken a year to create the airfield on the boggy terrain of Fairwood Common, as large quantities of industrial spoil were required to make the ground solid enough to build. Although voices were raised in favour of returning the site to common land, plans were put into place by the Swansea Corporation to convert the RAF station into a local airport.

The street plan was altered to create two broad thoroughfares in The Kingsway and Princess Way. The site of Ben Evans department store became Castle Gardens, and a new store for David Evans was built on its old site. In Castle Gardens a shelter was provided in the north-east corner, which proved very popular with older shoppers, but it was removed in a later revamp of the gardens. The Dragon Hotel was built on the site of the Old Gower Hotel and a large roundabout was created in front of it to link Orchard Street, College Street, Princess Way, The Kingsway and Belle Vue Way. This has now gone, with a large junction in its place. Princess Way has been pedestrianised for part of its route, and there have been a number of changes to The Kingsway and Orchard Street in recent years.

There was some urgency in the redevelopment of post-war Swansea and as a result some quite uninspiring buildings were erected. One of these was the Unifloc Building, which was built on a piece of land between Adelaide Street and Victoria Road. Very few people had anything good to say about this building, and as it was situated at one of the gateways to Swansea, it was eventually demolished in 2005. In its stead there is now a small car park and a landscaped garden area, which is in front of the Swansea Museum.

RAF Fairwood Common was created at the start of the Second World War to meet the requirement for more airfields. These fitters are working on the Rolls-Royce Merlin engine of a Boulton Paul Defiant of 125 Squadron RAF in January 1942.

Close by was the 1860 building that was the Swansea Harbour Trust offices, and next door was the Sailor's Home. This pair of buildings was on the corner of Mount Street and Victoria Road. However, the Harbour Trust only occupied their offices until 1903, when new offices were built a short distance away on Adelaide Street. These buildings continue in use today as Morgan's Hotel. The 1860 Harbour Trust offices and the Sailor's Home were demolished in 1964 to enable the creation of a dual carriageway.

Another 1960s-style office block that became redundant was Oldway House, just a little further along Oystermouth Road. In this instance the building had housed, among others, the Department of Social Security. When they left, the building, which was another that did not appeal aesthetically, was surplus to requirements and so demolished in 2013. At the same time a large part of the St David's Shopping Centre, which had become a bit of a white elephant, was taken away, and the whole site became a car park. I do not know if there are any firm plans to redevelop this site.

The Clarence Street car park was another structure declared to be ugly, and although it had been used quite regularly when there were games at the nearby Vetch Field, once that closed, it was felt the car park could be cleared away too. This happened in 2015.

On the other side of town, on the riverside near Parc Tawe, the Unit Superheater factory spread over quite a large area. When this was closed, the whole site was cleared, and currently student accommodation for the University of Wales Trinity

Oldway House. Swansea's cityscape is constantly changing, which is why I can feature so many lost buildings and other features. Oldway House, situated next to the St David's Shopping Centre, has become surplus to requirements. Part of the St David's Shopping Centre was considered to be a white elephant as the units could not be filled. As a result, both Oldway House and the unusable part of St David's Centre were demolished in 2012/13. The area has been turned into a car park. (Brian Prouton)

This postcard view of High Street, taken around 1905, shows just how bustling and busy this street was, crammed with shops, hotels and pubs. At the time, it was probably the main shopping street.

Wind Street was one of the original medieval streets of the town of Swansea. Once the first Norman castle had been built, a settlement comprising traders, craftsmen and others grew up. Wind Street was the first street to develop, mimicking as it did the course of the river. This explains the gentle curve of the street. By Victorian times, the street had become popular with banks wishing to establish local offices. Local newspaper *The Cambrian* established its offices here and it became the home of the Head Post Office. Along with shops and hotels, a wide variety of establishments centred on the street. Much of this has gone now, and Wind Street specialises in entertainment in the form of clubs, bars, restaurants, etc.

Oxford Street, *c*. 1905. Once the new market was established in Oxford Street in 1830, that street, too, attracted more shops and gradually became the premier shopping street that it is today. The building of the Quadrant Centre only served to pull the shopping heart of the city down to the Oxford Street area. This particular view is taken from a point close to today's Marks & Spencer store and looks across what is today Princess Way to Temple Street.

This photograph of Mayhill Farm dates from the early years of the twentieth century, well before it was taken over for municipal housing. The name lives on, of course, as the estate created is now called Mayhill.

Brynlliw Colliery. The Lower Swansea Valley was not the only area of Swansea to become industrialised. The reliance on coal as fuel meant that collieries sprang up all around the area. This photograph of Brynlliw Colliery in Grovesend is valuable as it shows the extent of the buildings needed on the surface to support a colliery.

Swansea Hospital. Founded in 1814 as the Swansea Dispensary, this building became the Swansea Infirmary from 1867 to 1872, then took the name Swansea Hospital up until 1889. As the Swansea General and Eye Hospital it provided care until 1948. Twenty years later it was closed and was replaced by the newly built Singleton Hospital. Converted into flats for older folk, it is now called Homegower House.

The Countess of Huntingdon's Chapel. The Countess of Huntingdon's Connexion was a Calvinistic movement within the Methodist Church, founded at the time of the eighteenth-century religious revival. The countess built chapels in a number of towns, and in Swansea her chapel was built in Herbert Place at the Burrows in 1782. The architect of the building was William Jernagen. It was enlarged in 1841 and again in 1877.

St David is being built there, along with some residential accommodation. More student accommodation is being built on the site of an Indian restaurant on Christina Street, just off The Kingsway.

Mention of the Vetch Field here gives me an opportunity to include some sporting changes in Swansea. The Vetch itself was last used for a Football League match on 30 April 2004. Swansea City AFC then moved to a new home at the Liberty Stadium at Morfa. The Vetch, although once earmarked for housing development, has become a community asset with part of it grassed over and part dedicated to the Vetch Veg Project, creating allotments and gardens for local people.

Morfa, of course, was the home of the Morfa Stadium, which was the base for the Swansea Harriers Athletics Club and was also used by local schools. In use from 1980, it was opened officially by Elizabeth II and the Duke of Edinburgh in 1989. The stadium was later demolished and replaced by the Liberty Stadium, the Morfa Retail Park and the Copper Quarter residential development.

The year 1989 also saw the creation of a dry ski slope at Morfa, which was in use up until 2008. The site is now abandoned and is an eyesore. The St Helen's Ground continues to host cricket matches, although rugby was also played there. On 22 March 1952, Wales played France in the last senior rugby international to be played in Swansea. Wales won 9-5. The photograph featured here was taken during the game by an unnamed French press photographer.

Swansea in the nineteenth century was an industrial powerhouse, and great wealth was accrued by those families who owned the works, the railways and the canals and all that which made the industrial processes possible. While it is said that with wealth comes responsibility, and many of these families were philanthropists, they were also keen to build for themselves impressive houses. The western suburbs of Swansea were by far the most appealing, being, as they were, away from the noxious air of the Lower Swansea Valley and not affected by the prevailing wind, which carried this unpleasant atmosphere over the eastern parts of the town.

Consequently, there are a number of important houses to be found around Sketty that date from the period between the 1750s and the 1850s. Sketty Hall was built in 1758. Sketty Park was built around 1806 by the Morris family, who had decided to demolish Clasemont House in that year, as the air quality was so bad in the Morriston area. Clasemont had been built around 1775, so it did not have a very long life. Sketty Park was demolished in 1975 at the time that the Sketty Park estate of municipal housing was being built. Hendrefoilan House and Singleton Abbey are both now part of the University of Swansea, as is Clyne Castle. The grounds of Clyne Castle were retained by the county borough council and are today the nationally renowned Clyne Gardens, known for its collection of rhododendrons.

Sketty Hall is now part of Gower College. Glynderwen House, Derwen Fawr and Sketty Isaf became the Bible College, the purpose of which was to train Christian missionaries for service overseas. From 1933, the Bible College provided a school for the children of missionaries, and it became so popular that Glynderwen House became its permanent home. Additional buildings and facilities were provided and in 1955 the Bible College School changed its name to Emmanuel Grammar School. Earlier, in 1939 the college had acquired the Penllergare estate, which included Penllergare House. After local government reorganisation in 1974, Lliw Valley District Council built their new Civic Centre on the site of Penllergare House, which had been demolished in the 1960s.

Holy Trinity Church. This church stood at the junction of Alexandra Road and Pleasant Street. Founded in 1843 as the mother church of the parish of Holy Trinity, it suffered bomb damage during the Second World War. After the war, and as the parish had been combined with St Mary's in 1936, the building was considered redundant. Demolished as a result, the site is now occupied by sheltered housing.

The last rugby international played in Swansea. On 22 March 1952, Wales played France in the last senior rugby international to be played in Swansea. Wales won 9-5. This photograph was taken by an unnamed French press photographer.

Dry ski slope at Morfa. Opened in 1989 and in use up to 2008, the site is now abandoned and has become an eyesore. Plans to open shops and restaurants on the site have not gone beyond discussion stage.

The land surrounding this building is now being developed for housing that will stretch from Cadle up to the edge of Penllergare Valley Woods. These woods have been saved for the community by fierce local action.

The year 1974 was the year of Local Government Reorganisation, with the creation of West Glamorgan County Council, within which there were four districts: Swansea, Lliw Valley, Afan and Neath. The creation of this new county council necessitated the building of a headquarters. The site chosen was around Paxton Street in Swansea, and included Dunvant Place and Sloane Street, as well as the Paxton Street Locomotive Depot. Built to reflect the maritime history of its host city and the seaside location, the building has the look of the upper superstructure of a ship. Subsequent further reorganisation of local government in Wales meant the demise of West Glamorgan County Council, and County Hall passed to the new unitary authority: the city and county of Swansea. Lliw Valley disappeared and was divided up between Swansea, and the other new unitary authority carved from West Glamorgan, which brought Neath and Port Talbot together as one. The old Lliw Valley Civic Centre passed to this authority.

Swansea Teacher Training College stood on Townhill, overlooking the town and the bay. The building has, over the years, been extended and adapted, as the requirements of teacher training have changed. Today it is part of the University of Wales Trinity St David. Another building that is part of that university is the old Grammar School on Mount Pleasant Hill. The original Grammar School had been founded by Bishop Hugh Gore in the 1682. The site on Mount Pleasant dates from 1853, and there were additional buildings added in 1869. In 1895 the school became the Swansea Intermediate and Technical School for Boys, with the old High School for Girls becoming the Intermediate and Technical School for Girls. Destruction in the Blitz meant that the Grammar School was moved to a new site in Sketty, on De-la-Beche Road, and was named Bishop Gore Grammar School. It is now a co-educational comprehensive school. Swansea no longer has any grammar schools.

The site on Mount Pleasant became Swansea Technical College and then the West Glamorgan Institute of Higher Education after 1974. In the 1990s moves were being made to encourage institutions of this type to adopt university status, and so it became Swansea Metropolitan University. Further reorganisation of Welsh higher education absorbed the Metropolitan University into the University of Wales Trinity St David, together with Trinity College Carmarthen and St David's University College Lampeter.

Education provision had been extended in 1883 when the Trinity Place Board School became a higher grade school for both boys and girls. The cramped conditions led to the boys being moved to a new location – Russell House in Dynevor Place. This site was expanded with the building of new classrooms and a gymnasium. The building on Dynevor Place became the Dynevor Secondary School for Boys and the building on De-la-Beche Street became the De-la-Beche Secondary School for Girls. Opening in 1929, the school received several hits during the Blitz, necessitating remedial works. The surviving buildings continued as a boys' school, then as a co-educational comprehensive school by amalgamating with Llwyn-y-Bryn Girls' School. Now closed as a school, the buildings are another element in the University of Wales Trinity St David. Llwyn-y-Bryn school buildings are now part of Gower College.

Swansea's Teacher Training College stood high above the town at Townhill. It underwent many extensions and adaptations as the nature of the teacher education it was required to give changed. It is now part of the University of Wales Trinity St David.

Before moving on, I just want to mention Oxford Street School, which was opened in 1848 as Oxford Street National School, being enlarged in 1909 and 1932. It survived the Blitz and became a secondary modern school. It closed as a school in 1969 and was for several years a teacher's resource centre. Demolition came in 1989, and the site is now a car park, partly to serve the Grand Theatre, which stands opposite. One other well-known Swansea school was the Glanmor Central School for Boys and Girls, which was founded in 1922 in wooden ex-army buildings. These served for fifty years, as the school, by then a girls-only school, closed in 1972. However, the buildings were not yet ready to retire, being called on again when they were brought back into use between 1974 and 1976 to house pupils from Olchfa School who had been evacuated because high alumina cement had been found on their modern campus. The site was cleared in 1989 to be used for housing.

In this survey of what Swansea has lost over the years, I have not been tempted to list every single pub, hotel or feature. I am sure many readers will be saying 'he hasn't included this pub or that house'. It would require a much longer book to include everything, and would involve more repetition than I have already indulged in. Swansea is a very different place than even eighty years ago, having suffered bombings by the Luftwaffe, town planning and architectural mistakes, and the dramatic decline of its industrial base. However, I hope that you have found it interesting, and that some memories have been rekindled.

Dynevor School after the Blitz. The De La Beche Street/Dynevor Place corner of Dynevor School had boasted three floors and a tower. This corner suffered more or less a direct hit during the Blitz and was destroyed. The top floor of the Dynevor building was damaged too. When repairs were carried out new classrooms were incorporated onto the top floors of both buildings, and a single-storey assembly hall was included in the corner. As a result there was no direct connection between the two buildings and staff and pupils had to make their way across the yard to change buildings.

Glanmor Girls' School. Founded as Glanmor Central School for Boys and Girls in 1922, the school became a girls-only establishment in 1941, when the boys' school was closed. The school buildings were wooden ex-army buildings, which served until the ultimate closure in 1972, when the school was amalgamated with Bishop Gore Comprehensive School. The wooden buildings actually served beyond that date, as they were brought back into use from 1974 to 1976 to house pupils from Olchfa Comprehensive School when high alumina cement was found on their modern campus. The site was cleared in 1989 and was used for housing.

Gowerton Primary School. Recently closed, the school buildings are currently standing empty but are up for sale.

Oxford Street School. Opened in 1848 as Oxford Street National School, it was enlarged in 1909 and 1932. It survived the Blitz, and after the war became a secondary modern school. Closed as a school in 1969, it became, for a while, a teachers' resources centre. Demolition came in 1989, and the site became a car park, principally for the Grand Theatre, which is situated opposite.

Gwydr Crescent, Uplands. I have included this 1905 postcard view of Gwydr Crescent because it shows vividly how a community can change over a century. Both sides of the road here are residential properties with the exception of the Uplands Hotel on the right-hand side. Today all these properties are retail or service outlets.

Sketty village. This superb postcard view of Sketty Cross was taken and published by Ernest T. Bush, a prolific local photographer and publisher. The Bush Inn can be clearly seen on the corner, although the Vivian Arms is hidden from view by buildings on the left that have long since gone. With just a few pedestrians and a couple of carts, life was clearly lived at a gentler pace then.

Broadway, Sketty. This view shows an open aspect quite different from the same view today. Broadway itself is now lined with mature trees, and the hillside beyond has been developed for housing.

Mumbles Road, *c.* 1905. Compare this with a similar view today! No traffic queues, although there is hardly any traffic. The road surface may not be up to current standards, and in dry weather dust was a problem.

Dunns, Mumbles. Plenty of people out and about enjoying good weather for a day out. The main difference, of course, is that they were able to come to Mumbles on the Mumbles Railway.

Parkmill got its name from the mill that served the Parc-le-Breos estate. The mill was placed where the river could run a watermill, and visitors can still see that arrangement. The site is now the Gower Heritage Centre, and is a popular tourist attraction.

Penrice Castle, Oxwich

Penrice Castle in this instance refers to the Georgian house built for the Talbot family, whose main residence was at Margam Abbey near Port Talbot. In the latter part of the nineteenth century a large wing, larger even than the original house, was added. In the 1970s, however, in order to reduce the financial burden of maintaining such a big property, the Victorian wing was demolished.

Acknowledgements

The preparation of this book would not have been possible without help from a number of people.

Firstly, I would like to thank the late Alan Jones, who had accumulated a superb collection of postcards and other images of Swansea, some of which appear in this book. Also I wish to thank Peter Muxworthy for permission to peruse his wonderful collection and borrow freely.

Thanks also to Bob Harris, who has lent me several photographs related to Swansea Docks, and to D. K. James for permission to reproduce his photograph of Victoria station. Also to Brian Davies for useful information on Gorseinon and Grovesend, and to Shona Small for advice.

Lastly, I must thank my family, especially my daughter Rebecca, whose help with the technical side of matters has been invaluable, and to my son Steffan and, of course, my wife Alicia. Also to Brian Prouton for his excellent line drawings.

Finally, can I just add that over the years I have collected hundreds of images of Swansea. These have been found in antique shops, charity shops and bookshops among other places. If I have used an image and failed to credit it, it is simply that I have forgotten where an image came from, or who had lent it to me. I apologise and will make the necessary amendments at the first opportunity.

Also available from Amberley Publishing

DAVID GWYNN

SWANSEA
HISTORY TOUR

A guided tour of the historic town of Swansea, showing how the areas
you know and love have changed over the centuries.

978 1 4456 7316 5

Available to order direct 01453 847 800

www.amberley-books.com

LOST
SWANSEA

DAVID GWYNN

AMBERLEY

First published 2019

Amberley Publishing
The Hill, Stroud
Gloucestershire, GL5 4EP

www.amberley-books.com

British Library Cataloguing in Publication Data.

A catalogue record for this book is available from the British Library.

ISBN 978 1 4456 9358 3 (print)
ISBN 978 1 4456 9359 0 (ebook)

Origination by Amberley Publishing.
Printed in the UK.